WHEN YOU RECEIVE THE
Aaronic Priesthood

Learning to Use the Keys, Powers, and Blessings

Eric G. Stephan & R. Wayne Pace

CFI
Springville, Utah

ISBN 13: 978-1-55517-902-9
ISBN 10: 1-55517-902-9
e. 1

Published by CFI, an imprint of Cedar Fort, Inc., 925 N. Main, Springville, UT, 84663
Distributed by Cedar Fort, Inc. www.cedarfort.com

LIBRARY OF CONGRESS CATALOGING-IN-PUBLICATION DATA

Stephan, Eric G.
  When you receive the Aaronic priesthood : learning to use the keys, powers, and blessings / Eric G. Stephan & R. Wayne Pace.
    p. cm.
  Includes bibliographical references and index.
  ISBN 1-55517-902-9 (alk. paper)
  1. Aaronic Priesthood (Mormon Church) I. Pace, R. Wayne. II. Title.

  BX8659.5.S74 2006
  262'.149332--dc22

                                              2006002151

Cover design by Nicole Williams
Cover design © 2006 by Lyle Mortimer
Printed in the United States of America

10   9   8   7   6   5   4   3   2   1

Printed on acid-free paper

Dedication

To all the young men of Aaronic Priesthood age throughout the far reaches of the Church. May they discover new insights and receive the spiritual strength that will make their lives more precious, more powerful, and more inspirational.

Contents

Acknowledgments

We express gratitude to the young men of the Church who have inquired so often about the real power and blessings of the Aaronic Priesthood. They have wondered what keys and power are associated with the Aaronic Priesthood and what they mean. We have attempted to respond to their concerns and talk to them in a direct but honest and friendly manner.

Early in the development of this book, we consulted several bishops and other Church leaders about what they thought should go into a book about the Aaronic Priesthood. We wish to acknowledge their influence on the direction and substance of this work. We trust that they will see the fruits of their inspiration.

We wish to acknowledge, of course, the steady influence of our wives, Sandra Utley Stephan and Gae Tueller Pace, on this work. Without their support, we could not possibly have produced a book of this significance and impact. We cherish their constant and continuing oversight.

Finally, we wish to acknowledge the efforts of Cedar Fort in bringing this effort to fruition and placing these ideas before the public.

Think of it! When you receive the Aaronic Priesthood, you join a mighty company of individuals who hold the priesthood. You are now counted among those to whom the Lord has given his power and authority to act in his name. Can you believe that? God himself has arranged to give you some of his authority to represent him and carry out his work on this earth. Most of the young men in the world have no authority to act for the Lord. But you are among those that do.

In addition, when you receive the Aaronic Priesthood you are given three important keys. These special keys will open up a whole new world of understanding to you. You will definitely want to take some time and learn how to use these keys to unlock great opportunities and blessings for you and help you become a more powerful servant of the Lord.

The Aaronic Priesthood has been restored to the earth for the benefit of the people living on the earth at this time. President Gordon B. Hinckley reported in the May 22, 2004, issue of *Church News* that there are "more than 300,000 Aaronic Priesthood holders working unitedly to advance the kingdom of God in the earth" right now.

Orson Pratt, a brilliant thinker and an early member of the Quorum of the Twelve Apostles (1835–1881) also enlarges our view of priesthood activity with a most fascinating observation. His insight emerged while serving as an apostle and as a professor at the University of Utah where he was regarded as a preeminent scholar in the field of higher mathematics.

Elder Pratt explained that "there are authorities in heaven as well as upon the earth, and the authorities in heaven are far greater in number than the few who are upon the earth. This is only a little branch of the great tree of the Priesthood—merely a small branch receiving authority from heaven, so that the inhabitants of the earth may be benefited as well as the inhabitants of the eternal world; but the great trunk of the tree of the Priesthood is in heaven. There you will find thousands and millions holding the power of the Priesthood" (*Masterful Discourses of Orson Pratt* [Salt Lake City: Bookcraft, 1962], 259).

When you receive the priesthood, you are joined with all holders of the priesthood, shoulder to shoulder, heart to heart, in receiving authority from heaven to benefit you as well as all the inhabitants of the world. The possibilities for your growth and development under the mantle of the priesthood are almost unimaginable. You should be thrilled and encouraged with the opportunities that now become yours, and you should reach out with all your might to claim these extraordinary blessings.

As individuals who have grown up in the Church and lived during the most dramatic increases in Church growth and development, we have encountered a full range of priesthood experiences. We can testify directly to the keys, powers, and blessings of the Aaronic Priesthood. We have also carefully studied numerous writings and discourses about the Aaronic Priesthood by the general authorities of the Church. We have included in this book some of the most important ideas about the Aaronic Priesthood explained by members of the First Presidency, the Quorum of the Twelve Apostles, the Presiding Bishopric, and the Seventy.

We will share the most vital of these understandings with you and your parents in this book. You may want to read this book with your parents, so they can help you understand better what our Church leaders are trying to tell you about the Aaronic Priesthood. We have made each chapter as short and clear as possible so that you can quickly catch on to each idea.

The best way to learn and remember an idea is to share it with someone. As quickly as you learn an idea, share it with a family member or a friend. That way, you will remember the idea longer and others will learn wonderful things from you.

If you have any doubts in your mind about what you should do with regard to receiving the priesthood and attending Church regularly, listen to this testimony of Oliver Cowdery about the Aaronic Priesthood. Oliver Cowdery was with Joseph Smith on the banks of the Susquehanna River when John the Baptist laid his hands upon their heads and restored the Aaronic Priesthood. Oliver Cowdery described what happened:

> While the world was racked and distracted—
> while millions were groping as the blind for the wall,
> and while all men were resting upon uncertainty, as
> a general mass, our eyes beheld—our ears heard. . . .
> Then his voice, though mild, pierced to the center,
> and his words, "I am thy fellow servant," dispelled all
> fear. We listened, we gazed, we admired! 'Twas the
> voice of an angel from glory, 'twas a message from
> the Most High. . . . Where was room for doubt?
> Nowhere; the uncertainty had fled, doubt had sunk
> no more to rise, while fiction and deception had fled
> forever! (*History of the Church* 1:43).

You don't have to wonder, doubt, or be confused about what to do or which direction to go with regard to your activity in the Church or receiving the priesthood. There is absolutely no doubt that the keys and blessings of the Aaronic Priesthood have been restored. All you have to do is learn more about the power and authority that you have and then use it in your daily life.

During the first part of this book, we will explain to you what it means to receive the priesthood and how to use it to benefit yourself and others. In the second part of this book, we will explain how to add significant power to the authority of the priesthood that you have received. And in the third part of the book, we will explain how to avoid some of the not-so-good things that happen at school and in the community that may weaken you as a holder of the priesthood.

As you read and ponder the powerful principles discussed in this book and put them into practice in your life, your faith and confidence will increase. You will become a stronger person, less likely to be pushed and shoved around, or intimidated by other people who don't understand the great truths of the gospel. Your understanding of the enormity, the splendor, and the glory of the Aaronic Priesthood will enlarge. And you will take your place among the wonderful people here and beyond who hold the priesthood and welcome its blessings.

Part I

What it Means to Receive the Aaronic Priesthood

Chapter 1

Congratulations, Twice!

First, congratulations because you became a member of The Church of Jesus Christ of Latter-day Saints when you were baptized by immersion by someone who had priesthood authority from God to baptize you. Immediately after your baptism, someone who had the Melchizedek Priesthood laid his hands upon your head and gave you the gift of the Holy Ghost. This is the greatest gift you can have here in mortality while you are away from your Heavenly Father. By trying to do what is right and being worthy of the gift of the Holy Ghost, you can always feel how much the Lord knows and loves you. You never have to feel alone. And by asking the Lord in faith, you can receive personal directions, promptings, and inspiration to make good and righteous decisions throughout your whole life.

Second, congratulations on receiving the Aaronic Priesthood! All men on this earth are children of Heavenly Father. But you have something more. You have authority to act in his name. This makes you different and distinguishes you from the rest of the world.

Because you know that you are a son of Heavenly Father and hold his priesthood, more will be expected of you than those who do not have this tremendous blessing. The first thing you must do is become aware of the sacredness of your ordination and calling in the Aaronic Priesthood. President Thomas S. Monson explained how that awareness happened to him:

> In my life, this was accomplished when the bishopric asked that I take the sacrament to a shut-in who lived about a mile from the chapel. That special Sunday morning, as I knocked on the door of Brother Wright and heard his feeble reply, "Come in," I entered not only his humble cottage but also a room filled with the Spirit of the Lord. I approached his bedside and carefully placed a piece of bread to his lips. I then held the cup of water that he might drink. As I departed, I saw him smile as he said, "God bless you, my boy." And God did bless me with an appreciation for the sacred emblems which continues even today. ("The Aaronic Priesthood Pathway," *Ensign*, November 1984, 41)

President Monson became aware of the sacredness of his calling in the priesthood by using his authority to serve someone. Your first job is to learn your duties as an Aaronic Priesthood holder, start to serve others, and magnify your callings. Your parents will help you. Your quorum advisors will help you. Your quorum presidency will help you. The bishopric will help you. Your home teachers and your faithful friends who hold the Aaronic Priesthood will help you. You will have plenty of help to learn your duties and keep you strong as you become a faithful priesthood holder.

If you look around at young men your age, you will probably see many boys who lie, cheat, and treat others unfairly. We sometimes say that boys stumble and falter along the path, but we mean that they're doing the wrong things. For you to avoid getting lost along the path from deacon to teacher to priest to the Melchizedek Priesthood, to avoid getting sidetracked by various snares and temptations, it is most important for you to stay close to the ward leadership of the Aaronic Priesthood. Talk frequently to your leaders. Listen carefully to them. Do what they say. And try your hardest to be a good representative of the Lord Jesus Christ himself.

Knowledge is power! You must fortify and strengthen yourself by getting as much knowledge about the Aaronic Priesthood as you can. Read and ponder the topics discussed in this book. Listen carefully to the lessons you receive in your priesthood meeting. If you have any questions about what you read or what you hear, ask your parents, quorum advisor, or bishop.

Our promise is that if you study and do the work of the Aaronic Priesthood, you will have the kind of experience that Heavenly Father has planned for you while you live on this earth. Remember that Heavenly Father knows you personally. You are his son. He knows your name. Like your own earthly father, Heavenly Father will do anything that he can to help you live a good life and return to his presence.

Your Heavenly Father tends to work through your earthly father, mother, bishop, and priesthood leaders to give you help. Pay attention to what they have to say, and you'll feel the inspiration of your Father in Heaven. That is how it works. You're off to a good start; keep moving in the right direction.

Chapter 2

Getting through Turbulent and Exciting Times

One of Elder Boyd K. Packer's sons received a colt as a gift when he was about your age. The colt ran wild with horses on the boy's grandfather's ranch, but by the time it was two years old, it had grown enough to start the taming process.

Late in the spring, the boy and his family went to the ranch and wrangled the horses into a corral. They put the boy's horse in a chute with a halter on it and tied it to a big post. Elder Packer told his son that the horse had to stay there three days until it quit fighting and settled down. They worked with the horse during the morning, and then they went inside for lunch. The boy hurried through his meal and went back outside to see his horse. The boy loved the horse, but the boy was only fourteen.

Just as the family finished lunch, they head a scuffling noise and a muffled shout. They knew what had taken place. The boy had untied the horse and planned to work with it to speed up the taming process. To hold the horse, the boy had wrapped the rope around his wrist. As the whole family rushed out the kitchen door, they saw the horse trot past. The boy was running alongside the horse, taking giant steps to keep up, and then he stumbled and fell. Fortunately, the horse was cornered between two fences, slowing its pace but still dragging the boy. While the horse was trying to find its way out of the fenced area, the family members reached the animal, removed the rope from the boy's wrist, and tied it around a fence post. The boy was bruised but not badly hurt.

The boy was frightened, and his father wondered what they should do next. After some consoling words, the two decided to train the horse gradually. So, over a period of two years, they used a bucket of oats and much kindness to prepare the horse for riding. In the spring of the third year, they went to the ranch, took a bucket of oats, and walked to the edge of the meadow where the horses were feeding. The other horses, sensing their presence, started to move away, but the boy whistled and his horse came out of the herd and trotted up to him. The horse had been prepared, and the boy had learned an important lesson (see "A Priesthood of Preparation," *New Era,* May 1979, 42).

What did the boy learn? If you thought he learned that he couldn't tame and train his horse in only a few days, you're right. And so it is with you, and with all of us. If we are doing little things that don't work for us and we're perfectly aware of what to change that would make our life better, we can usually make that change rather quickly.

But growth and development always take a little longer. For example, growing from a young twelve-year-old into a confident and knowledgeable nineteen-year-old will take more than a few weeks. Receiving the Aaronic Priesthood and then learning to use its full power and keys is going to take a little time. Fortunately, this journey of learning will be one of the most exciting things that you do in your whole life.

If you're a normal young person, you'll want to go faster and quicker than your wisdom and experience can securely take you. However, much like the young boy who wanted to ride his horse before it had been trained, you must develop patience as well as persistence to successfully survive and adjust to this twelve-to-nineteen-year-old period of time in your life. Remember that things of great value come a little slower, but they are worth the time and effort required to receive them. Someone said, "Inch by inch, life's a cinch. Yard by yard, life is hard." Some of the greatest blessings and powers of the priesthood that you hold come quickly while other blessings and powers may take a little longer.

With these admonitions in mind, we would personally like to welcome you to one of the most exiting and challenging times in your life—those years from twelve to nineteen years when you are moving from a young man to a responsible adult. Your body changes, your thinking changes, your feelings about right and wrong may become confused, your interests change, and even the clothes you wear change.

If you are a normal young man, you may sometimes feel wobbly and unsure of yourself. You may think you're doing fine when all of a sudden, life reminds you that you're not doing as well as you think you are. In fact, sometimes you may do something wrong, feel quite uncomfortable because you did it, and not even know why you did it in the first place!

You should be aware of something else. You may not have noticed it, but during the past few years, we have seen staggering increases in crime, gang activity, drug use, teenage pregnancy, homicide, violence, abuse, lying, cheating, pornography, filthy language, beer and alcohol use, connecting with the wrong people on the Internet, and a growing disregard for the lives and property of others.

Just look at the daily newspaper or watch local TV news programs and you may be surprised at how people are mistreating one another and doing things that bring jail sentences and fines rather than freedom, opportunity, and happiness. Even when you look around at school or in your community, you'll see many people your own age doing the wrong things.

The sad part is that if you're not careful, you'll be dragged into this turbulence, and you won't even know it until it's almost too late to do anything about it. Nephi described the times in which you are living. He said: "For behold, at that day shall he [the devil] rage in the hearts of the children of men, and stir them up to anger against that which is good" (2 Nephi 28: 20–21).

Pay more attention to how many times you feel a little upset at being told what to do when your parents or teachers try to teach you to do something that is good. Do you act like the horse in the chute and get a little worked up and try to get away from the person trying to help you? Do you find yourself getting stirred up against that which is good? And the biggest question of all: Is there a way to get through this next year or two and cope with all the subtle changes that are taking place within you and around you?

Fortunately the answer is an emphatic *Yes!*

Listen carefully: There is no remedy that is more effective at your present age than to receive the Aaronic Priesthood and learn how to use its keys, powers, and blessings. Every modern and ancient faithful priesthood holder that has done so has been led and directed through difficult times to a happier way of living. You can do the same.

When young men move away from these sacred powers, they frequently become confused and soon try to replace peace of mind and joy with various kinds of activities that give them only a sense of temporary pleasure and pride. Indeed, it almost seems like the farther they move away from the powers and blessings of the priesthood, the more they are left to the temptations, confusion, and calamities of the modern world and, like Elder Packer's son, are dragged across the corral until someone rescues them.

Elder Boyd K. Packer said in a recent general conference that you are part of a new generation. If you band together with other good people, you will be stronger than the previous generation and will do just fine ("The Least of These," *Ensign,* November, 2004, 87).

Receiving the Aaronic Priesthood is a truly momentous occasion in your life. All of the members of the ward will raise their hands and sustain you in your new calling. As you advance from deacon to teacher to priest, you will learn more and more about the significance of the power that you hold.

Remember, nothing of great value comes to any of us instantly. You must be patient and yet persistent. At the same time, you will be tempted and challenged by things that are going wrong around you. Even your friends may at times try to get you to do things that are wrong. That's when you need to band together with other good people, stay close to your family, and strengthen yourself by learning how to use the great priesthood powers and keys that you have.

We encourage you to read and learn all you can about the Aaronic Priesthood, think more about it, and then implement some principle or practice that you have learned into your life. Every correct idea you implement in your life will move you forward. And you will be surprised at how the windows of heaven are opened to you. You will receive blessings and guidance that you never dreamed of. Watch how quickly some of the insecurities and discomforts in your life disappear when you do the right things.

You have probably already noticed that when you do the right thing, you feel peaceful and happy. When you do the wrong thing, you feel uncomfortable, definitely not too peaceful, and not very happy. This is your opportunity to become one of the most happy and confident young men in the whole world. Just keep learning about the Aaronic Priesthood duties, powers, and blessings, and you will be on the safe path to an absolutely incredible journey of service and joy. This is exactly the kind of life that Heavenly Father has in mind for you.

Chapter 3

Why Is May 15, 1829, Important to You?

Let's begin at the beginning and discuss what is so important about May 15, 1829. While Joseph Smith and Oliver Cowdery were translating the Book of Mormon from the gold plates, they came across numerous references to baptism for the remission of sins, among which was the following:

"And again the Lord called others, and said unto them likewise; and he gave them power to baptize. And he said unto them: On this wise shall ye baptize; and there shall be no disputations among you. . . . Having authority given me of Jesus Christ, I baptize you in the name of the Father, and of the Son, and of the Holy Ghost. Amen" (3 Nephi 11:22, 25).

The Lord further instructed his leaders to stand in the water with the repentant person, immerse them in the water, and then come forth again out of the water.

These passages stirred deep feelings in Joseph and Oliver, creating in them a desire to be properly baptized into the kingdom of God. They also wondered who had authority to baptize and how baptism was to be done. They decided to ask the Lord. They found a small grove of trees on the bank of the Susquehanna River, near Joseph Smith's residence in Harmony, Pennsylvania, where they could pray in private.

As they started to pray, a most marvelous and incredible thing happened. Right there, near the cool, flowing waters of the river on a beautiful spring day in May, Joseph Smith and Oliver Cowdery clearly heard and felt the voice of the Lord speak to them. Then an angel of the Lord appeared before them.

The angel introduced himself as John the Baptist, who held the keys of baptism in the days of Jesus of Nazareth. He said that he was acting under the direction of Peter, James, and John, who held the keys of the priesthood of Melchizedek. When John the Baptist appeared to Joseph and Oliver, he was then a resurrected being. Joseph and Oliver could feel his hands on their heads when he gave them the priesthood.

Each Sunday in many wards throughout The Church of Jesus Christ of Latter-day Saints, priesthood holders meet together. Before they separate into quorums, a young man holding the Aaronic Priesthood stands up and leads the priesthood brethren in repeating aloud section 13 of the Doctrine and Covenants, which says:

> Upon you my fellow servants, in the name of Messiah I confer the Priesthood of Aaron, which holds the keys of the ministering of angels, and of the gospel of repentance, and of baptism by immersion for the remission of sins; and this shall never be taken again from the earth, until the sons of Levi do offer again an offering unto the Lord in righteousness.

Saying this scripture aloud with other priesthood holders is a tremendous experience. Everyone stands up and participates with a good deal of enthusiasm. John spoke the same words that we stand and repeat each Sunday in our priesthood meeting, and he conferred on Joseph and Oliver the same priesthood—with its keys, powers, and blessings—that was conferred upon you when you received the Aaronic Priesthood.

You may wonder why the priesthood that John conferred was called the priesthood of Aaron. Who was Aaron and why was the lower priesthood named after him? The answer is that Aaron was the older brother of Moses. The Lord gave incredible power to Aaron and appointed him to be a spokesman for Moses. During the Israelite departure from Egypt, Aaron was Moses' main assistant. Aaron came from the tribe of Levi, and his tribe was given various elements of the priesthood to be passed on through all of their future generations. This lesser portion of the higher priesthood is known as the Aaronic or Levitical Priesthood. When Aaron died, his priesthood authority was passed on not only to his sons but, down through the generations of time, to all those who are worthy of it.

Jesus said, "There is not a greater prophet than John the Baptist" (Luke 7:28). John gave Joseph and Oliver the same authority, the Aaronic Priesthood, which he had used when he baptized Jesus in the waters of the River Jordan. Can you understand why Joseph and Hyrum were so happy and amazed?

After almost two thousand years, this authority to teach repentance and administer baptism, to receive the ministering of angels, and to act in God's name, was restored once more to the earth. Think of it! Hands have been laid upon your head, and all of these same keys, powers, blessings, and authority have been given directly to you! As you continue reading, you may be surprised to learn about the numerous blessings and opportunities that you enjoy now because you hold the Aaronic Priesthood.

When you first receive the Aaronic Priesthood, you most likely feel a little anxious, yet excited, about the priesthood authority that you have received, even though you may not understand much about it. You realize that when you come to Church, you can participate in new ways. You can help with the sacrament, help the bishop collect fast offerings, help with home teaching, attend quorum meetings, and participate in numerous other priesthood activities. You feel more willing to come to Church and learn how to use this special authority that you have received. You feel more important and more appreciated. And as long as you keep doing what is right, these righteous feelings will always be with you.

It is especially impressive to note that according to section 13, as a recipient of the Aaronic Priesthood you hold the "keys of the ministering of angels." Can you believe that? According to President Gordon B. Hinckley, that means that you have the right "to enjoy the wonderful gifts, guidance, and protection which come therefrom" ("The Aaronic Priesthood—A Gift from God," *Ensign,* May 1988, 45–46). You have the wonderful opportunity to have heavenly messengers help you make good decisions, eliminate some of the confusion in your life, and protect you from harm and evil.

How much do you appreciate and understand the marvelous powers and blessings of the Aaronic Priesthood? We asked some young men a few questions:

- How are you different from those who don't hold the Aaronic Priesthood?
- What are the three keys of the Aaronic Priesthood, and how do you use them?
- What special powers and blessings are you now eligible to receive?
- Why did an angel have to restore the Aaronic Priesthood?
- What led up to the events that occurred on May 15, 1829?

The faces of some of the young men we questioned seemed blank and puzzled. If you just received the Aaronic Priesthood, you may be a little like these young men. You may have a vague idea about the answers to the questions but lack an understanding of the specifics. You may understand that you are different now from your nonmember friends, but you may not comprehend exactly why. As a result, you may not have quite the faith and confidence that comes as you learn more about the Aaronic Priesthood. And you may not know how to fully use your priesthood powers to benefit yourself and to help others. Remember what we said earlier:

Be patient in your learning, but be persistent. Continue now to the next chapter and pay particular attention to all the ways that the Aaronic Priesthood can help you live a happier life and be of greater service to those around you who need your support and encouragement.

Chapter 4

How the Aaronic Priesthood Can Help You

Could you use a little help in learning more about the priesthood, accomplishing your schoolwork, and being successful in other wholesome activities? Read what President Gordon B. Hinckley says about you:

"I love the boys who hold the Aaronic Priesthood. Every young man who does so, walking in obedience to the commandments of the Lord, may expect to have the guidance of the Holy Spirit in his life. That Spirit will bless him in his studies and other pursuits and will lead him in efforts that will bless him and bless the lives of others all about him" ("The Aaronic Priesthood—A Gift from God," *Ensign*, May 1988, 46).

This promise by a prophet is that as a holder of the Aaronic Priesthood who walks in obedience to the commandments, you will have the Holy Spirit to (1) bless you in your studies and other righteous activities and (2) lead you in efforts that will bless you and the lives of others all around you. That seems like reason enough for wanting to hold the Aaronic Priesthood and keep the commandments. But there is much more.

One Sunday afternoon in sacrament meeting, a returned missionary was reporting on his missionary experience. He testified with deep conviction that the gospel was true and that he had seen many miracles take place that made it possible for the missionaries to find, teach, and baptize investigators into the Church. Near the end of his talk, he looked over the congregation, focused on the young people, and said in a rather loud voice, "I love the Aaronic Priesthood!" He briefly explained how the Aaronic Priesthood had affected his life when he was searching for a testimony, how important it was to honor the Aaronic Priesthood by serving others, and how it opens the door to a happier life and the opportunity to go on a mission later on.

After the sacrament meeting ended, this young returned missionary was asked why he had spoken so strongly about the Aaronic Priesthood. He replied that the Aaronic Priesthood had literally saved his life, and he proceeded to tell this story:

"Unlike some young men in the Church, receiving the Aaronic Priesthood wasn't just another step on the ladder to exaltation for me, it was much, much more. At the age of eleven, I was left somewhat to fend for myself as far as the gospel goes. I was in and out of church from the age of eleven to twelve. Not having a solid testimony of the Church at this point in my life left me bewildered and somewhat adrift. I was searching though and really wanted to know if the gospel was true.

"While I was searching, I turned twelve years old and was to receive the Aaronic Priesthood. Even though I didn't understand much about it, I was found worthy and given the opportunity to receive the Aaronic Priesthood and be ordained a deacon. From that point on, my life seemed to change completely. Receiving the

Aaronic Priesthood was a call to duty. I felt drawn to the Church, and I sensed the necessity of serving in it. The responsibility of having the Aaronic Priesthood drove me to attend church each Sunday. The power of the priesthood was edifying to me, and the question of active church attendance faded from my mind.

"Many times the keys of the Aaronic Priesthood were manifest in my life. Especially in times of trial and confusion, the keys of the ministering of angels were used in behalf of me and my family. When alone or lost I would pray and then feel the closeness of these messengers. I felt comforted and understood what I needed to do to make things better in my own life and in the lives of other members of my family. I love the Aaronic Priesthood because it gave me direction and hope when I needed it most. The Aaronic Priesthood is an untapped source of power, and young people must recognize the power that they have and learn how to use it to its fullest extent."

Your parents may have heard of Elder James E. Talmage. He was a member of the Quorum of the Twelve Apostles during the early 1900s and a gifted writer who wrote *Jesus the Christ* and *The Articles of Faith,* books that are still used extensively throughout the Church today. As you read his remarks on how the Aaronic Priesthood helped him as a youth, notice particularly the tremendous source of strength the priesthood was to him outside of regular Church and quorum meetings:

> As soon as I had been ordained, a feeling came to me such as I have never been able to fully describe. It seemed scarcely possible, that I, a little boy, could be so honored of God as to be called to the priesthood. . . . I felt strong in the thought that I belonged to the Lord, and that he would assist me in whatever was required of me. The effect of my ordination [as a deacon] entered into all the affairs of my boyish life. I am afraid that sometimes I forgot what I was, but I have ever been thankful that ofttimes I did remember, and the recollection always served to make me better.

When at play on the school grounds and perhaps tempted to take unfair advantage in a game, when in the midst of a dispute with a playmate, I would remember, and the thought would be effective as though spoken aloud—"I am a deacon; and it is not right that a deacon should act this way."

On examination days, when it seemed easy for me to copy some other boy's work . . . I would say in my mind, "It would be more wicked for me to do that than it is for them, because I am a deacon." The impression made upon my mind when I was made a deacon has never faded. The feeling that I was called to the special service of the Lord, as a bearer of the priesthood, has been a source of strength to me through all the years. (*Incidents from the Lives of Our Church Leaders* (Deacon Instruction Manual) [Salt Lake City: The Church of Jesus Christ of Latter-day Saints, 1914], 135–36)

When you receive the Aaronic Priesthood, you become different from what you used to be. The Lord is going to share some of his power and authority with you. He is going to let you do sacred things now that you couldn't do before. You are now able to not only help others but also to realize great blessings in your own life.

You should realize also that not a single young man outside The Church of Jesus Christ of Latter-day Saints has the Aaronic Priesthood or authority to speak or act in the name of the Lord. No matter how powerful any president, king, or ruler of any country in the world is, none of them has the authority to even prepare, bless, and pass the sacrament. They must first receive the Aaronic Priesthood, as you did, before they have the proper authority.

The Lord loves you and has provided a way for you to become a member of his Church—The Church of Jesus Christ of Latter-day Saints. But, not only that, you have also been given the awesome privilege of holding the Aaronic Priesthood, with its accompanying keys, powers, and blessings. God has given you divine authority to act in the name of the Savior of all mankind. The Lord trusts you to always remember who you are, so that you don't bring dishonor to the priesthood that has been shared with you.

So there you have it. Now you know about the important event of May 15, 1829, and the multitude of ways the Aaronic Priesthood can help you. You also know why you should continue to learn how to use the significant powers that are contained within the priesthood. As you continue to read this book, you will learn more about the three keys of the Aaronic Priesthood and how you can use those for your benefit and the benefit of others.

Chapter 5

What Three Keys of the Aaronic Priesthood Do You Hold?

When you receive the Aaronic Priesthood, you receive certain unique keys, powers, and blessings. John the Baptist laid his hands upon the heads of Joseph Smith and Oliver Cowdery and gave them these same keys, powers, and blessings. John didn't use many words, but he said all that was important to carry out the great work of the Aaronic Priesthood. Read what John the Baptist said and see if you can identify the three keys given to you when you received the Aaronic Priesthood:

> Upon you my fellow servants, in the name of Messiah, I confer the Priesthood of Aaron, which

holds the keys of the *ministering of angels*, and of the
gospel of repentance, and of *baptism by immersion* for
the remission of sins; and this shall never be taken
again from the earth until the sons of Levi do offer
again an offering unto the Lord in righteousness.
(D&C 13; emphasis added)

According to this scripture, the three keys you receive when
you receive the Aaronic Priesthood are:
1. The ministering of angels.
2. The gospel of repentance.
3. Baptism by immersion for the remission of sins.

John the Baptist did a superb job of simplifying the
responsibilities of the Aaronic Priesthood. The three keys that
he restored and which were given to you when you received the
Aaronic Priesthood are specific blessings and rights that you
now have as a fellow servant of the Lord. These keys are put into
action as soon as you are called by a person with authority. The
important thing is to be worthy to use these keys as you hold and
exercise the priesthood of God.

As you know, keys unlock doors, chests, and other things
that can be locked. Keys usually unlock and reveal something
concealed. In this sense, President Gordon B. Hinckley said:
"What are keys? They represent the authority to unlock and make
available certain specific and wonderful blessings including the
ministering of angels" ("Upon You My Fellow Servants," *Tambuli*,
May 1989, 2; emphasis added).

You now have a most valuable resource to use for yourself
and your fellow man. Your goal should be to seek to understand
these keys and blessings and live worthy to use them.

Let's discuss each key separately.

First Key: The Ministering of Angels

The key of the ministering angels is one of the most exciting
keys of the Aaronic Priesthood because it puts you in touch
with heavenly beings. Every young man who holds the Aaronic

Priesthood is entitled to the ministering of angels. President Hinckley said, "That means that he [the Aaronic Priesthood holder] may call upon divine power for protection, for guidance, for comfort, for strength."

Who Are Angels?

Angels are individuals whom God sends to minister to us, instruct us, protect us, guide us in his work, support us, warn us, deliver messages, restore priesthood and keys, and perform all work necessary to accomplish the Lord's purposes. They are premortal, postmortal, or resurrected beings.

What Do Angels Do?

The scriptures speak frequently and plainly about the various kinds of work that angels do. For example, the angel Gabriel (Noah) was sent by the Lord to Zacharias to speak to him, bring him glad tidings, and tell him to give his new son the name John (Luke 1:11–14). When Peter was in prison, an angel caused the chains to fall off Peter's hands and led Peter out of prison. Herod was displeased with Peter's escape and gave an oration to his people, acting as though he was speaking for God. That was not a good thing to do! An angel quickly smacked him, and "he was eaten of worms, and gave up the ghost" (Acts 12:23).

When Paul was taken prisoner aboard a ship near Crete and the ship was threatened with destruction, the Lord sent an angel to instruct Paul how to stabilize the ship long enough for everybody on board to leave the ship alive (Acts 27:13–14, 21–25). The scriptures also confirm that angels may be seen or unseen while accomplishing their work, noting that "some have entertained angels unawares" (Hebrews 13:2).

Wilford Woodruff received the ministering of angels when he was a priest. He was marked to be killed by an apostate of the Church. His life was saved by divine intervention in a most dramatic way. After trying to visit and talk with a Mr. Akeman, Wilford Woodruff left his house. Mr. Akeman followed him, intending to harm him. At a point just outside the house,

Akeman fell dead as though he had been struck by a thunderbolt from heaven. Wilford Woodruff said later of the incident that he had received the administration of angels (*A Remarkable Life*, comp. Clair Ellen Koltko et al. [Springville, Utah: Cedar Fort, 2006], 56–60).

Angels may minister to a person, but that person may not understand where the warning, direction, or comfort comes from. A person may receive help, as Wilford Woodruff did, or guidance while trying to make critical decisions or even when speaking in Church or performing work in the temple. Sometimes, someone else may be aware of the presence of angels, even while the party being helped is unaware of their presence. Ask around and you may be surprised how many faithful Latter-day Saints know stories about the ministering of angels.

The point is you have the right to expect angels to help you today just as they have helped people in the past. If you are prepared, faithful in your calling, trying to live a good life, and serving others, you can claim such experiences because you have been given the keys to the ministering of angels, which means that you can open the door to this wonderful blessing.

The Second Key: THE GOSPEL OF REPENTANCE

Along with the keys of the administering of angels, you have also received the key of the gospel of repentance. You have the right to preach and teach the gospel and to have the support of the Lord in doing so. As soon as you understand the principles of the gospel, you should prepare yourself to explain those principles to others and to defend the Church and its doctrines. As an Aaronic Priesthood holder, you hold the keys and the authority to help others live a happier life.

By holding this second key of the Aaronic Priesthood, you acquire increased confidence and power to share your testimony and influence others for good. This key offers marvelous opportunities to magnify your calling as a priesthood holder, because many of your friends, schoolmates, and even family members feel like they are living in a troubled, confusing world.

You can influence them in a positive way by sharing the benefits and joys of living a more Christlike life. As you advance in various offices in the Aaronic Priesthood, you should prepare yourself for a mission and to receive the Melchizedek Priesthood. At that point, you will have an opportunity to join the tens of thousands of full-time missionaries who are taking the message of hope, peace, and happiness to all the nations of the world!

Prepare yourself to implement this key by living the gospel, by being a good example of a follower of Christ, and by taking every opportunity to teach the gospel in such a way that listeners will want to change their lives.

Don't simply tell someone to repent, rather share your standards with them and explain the incredible things that you feel when participating in Church meetings and services.

If your friends want to do something wrong, speak up and suggest a better activity.

E-mail your friends and tell them you have been thinking about them and want to share a great lesson or experience you've had in Church that helped you live a happier life.

When you become a home teacher, you will have regular opportunities to help members of the Church improve their lives as you share gospel thoughts and your testimony with them. Giving talks in church also allows you to exercise this key.

Don't hesitate to speak up and help others make their lives happier. You have the authority, you hold the key of the gospel of repentance, and the Lord will help you magnify your priesthood calling in this regard.

The Third Key: Baptism by Immersion

Listen to what President Hinckley has to say about this third key:

> As all of you who are priests know, you have the authority to baptize by immersion for the remission of sins. Have you ever thought of the wonder of that power? If a man or woman has truly repented of his or her sins, then he or she may be eligible to

be baptized by immersion with the understanding that those sins will be forgiven and that life can begin anew. It is no small or unimportant thing to baptize an individual. You as a young priest, acting in the name of the Lord and under divine authority, wipe out, as it were, by the marvelous process of baptism, the sins of the past and bring about a birth into a new and better life. What a tremendous responsibility you have to live worthy of the exercise of this sacred power! ("The Priesthood of Aaron," *Ensign*, November 1982, 44)

All knowledgeable members of the Church know that baptism is the primary ordinance of the gospel. It is the gate through which all must pass to be admitted into the Church. In fact, baptism by immersion is so important that it is performed not only for the living but for those who have passed away and live beyond the veil of death. Most young people who go to the temple and are baptized for those who have died bear a remarkable testimony about the Spirit of the Lord that is always there, witnessing the sacredness of this ordinance.

You hold keys and authority directly from God to act in his name. If you learn to use these keys well, you will find it much easier to overcome the power of Satan, of which some forms are discouragement, rebellion, and confusion. You will find yourself more in harmony with those in authority, closer to the Lord, and more confident that you are moving in the right direction to serve as a missionary, be married in the temple, and assume responsibilities of leadership in your family and in the Church.

Remember that the prophet holds the keys to these amazing blessings and opportunities. He gives these keys to you through the bishop of your ward. Stay close to the bishop.

Chapter 6

Your Connection to Your Bishop

Most of the time, ward members see the bishop sitting on the stand during sacrament meeting as the presiding ward leader. For many young people, he seems to not only be sitting quite a distance away, but he also seems involved with so many other members of the ward that he might not notice them. Until you become a holder of the Aaronic Priesthood, you may not even be aware of the personal concern and special relationship your bishop has with you.

Although the office and calling of the bishop is important to each member of the ward, his calling has a special significance to you. The Lord says that the bishop is the president of the Aaronic

Priesthood and president of the priest's quorum. He is the highest officer in the Aaronic Priesthood in your ward. The bishop is also the presiding high priest in the ward and has many responsibilities dealing with all the members of the ward (D&C 107:87–88).

However, he has some specific responsibilities where you, a holder of the Aaronic Priesthood, are concerned. As president of the Aaronic Priesthood, your bishop has the responsibility and obligation to give you his personal attention. The Lord has given your bishop special keys, powers, and insights so that you have a friendly, understanding man to be your personal helper and leader. Your bishop is there to listen to you, help you, guide you, keep your trust and confidence, and strengthen you in your relationship with the Lord.

Never feel intimidated by your bishop. He will be reaching out to you and paying personal attention to how you are doing in your life. Help him understand you. When you talk to your bishop and follow his counsel, you will discover that you are never feel alone or unwanted.

When Elder Robert D. Hales was the Presiding Bishop of the Church, he said:

> The best personal relationship I had with the youth came when we trusted each other and had open communication. For example, I developed an approach which required the participation of the young men in determining their worthiness to participate in the administration of the sacrament. We discussed the sacrament as a holy ordinance and the obligation Aaronic Priesthood holders have to be worthy in order to administer it.
>
> Instead of leaving the burden of who wasn't worthy to participate on the bishop's shoulders, I asked each deacon, teacher, or priest to come to me and let me know when they were not worthy. Then we worked together to solve their problem before it grew bigger. We had a good relationship, built on trust." ("The Bishop," *New Era*, June 1986, 42)

You can do several things to help your bishop help you, including:

1. Say hello to your bishop each Sunday. A cheery "Hi, Bishop" is the single best thing that a bishop likes to hear from you. The worst thing that you can do is ignore the bishop and walk past him. Simply saying *hello* or *hi* is a simple act of kindness and courtesy but has such a wonderful impact on both the bishop and you.

2. Occasionally make an appointment with your bishop to visit about questions you have, about your goals in life, or about anything in your life that causes you concern. Don't wait until you have made terrible mistakes before you talk to the bishop. He is your spiritual advisor, counselor, and friend, and you can make your life a lot happier by talking to him from time to time.

3. Whenever you have a chance, introduce your less-active friends or nonmember friends to your bishop. Let them feel of his deep love, great spirit, and concern for them. This is a simple way for you to share the gospel with your friends and enhance your relationship with your bishop.

4. Invite the bishop to your youth activities, quorum meetings, or classes. Although the bishop is assigned to be in the priests quorum on Sundays, he would like to know that you want him with you on other occasions. When you have a chance to be with the bishop as a group or class, prepare questions and identify specific concerns ahead of time that you would like the bishop to discuss.

Don't forget that your bishop can make your life less confusing and much happier as you seek his counsel. Young men have gone into their bishops' offices with what seemed like the weight of the world on their backs and come out smiling and with new hope. This is one of your great blessings and opportunities as an Aaronic Priesthood holder. Use it wisely.

Now we come to the moment of truth. Many young men will not take the time to build a good relationship with their bishop. Will you? Sometimes young men criticize or ignore their bishop. Do you? Many young people stand up, support the bishop, and seek out his counsel. Do you?

Your bishop will meet with you at important times in your life. He will interview you when you are ready to be ordained to a new office. He will regularly talk to you about your goals and aspirations, as well as your efforts to understand the full power and blessings of the priesthood. He will meet with you and your family at tithing settlement. When you are sick, he will comfort you. He will judge your worthiness to become an elder, go on a mission, and be married in the temple. Stay close to your bishop.

Your bishop has many assignments. You have the responsibility to help the bishop by carrying out your assignments. The bishop should be able to depend on you. With your help, not only does the work of the Lord move ahead but you as an individual are blessed, supported, lifted up, and encouraged—great blessings for a young man trying to live and survive happily in today's somewhat confusing world.

Now that you have an understanding of what the bishop has to do with the Aaronic Priesthood and with you, and you know several specific ways to build a stronger relationship with your bishop, let's take a few minutes to understand why every Aaronic Priesthood holder belongs to a quorum.

Chapter 7

You Are Part of a Quorum

As the Lord restored the gospel in these latter days and organized his Church, he organized the priesthood of the Church into quorums. A man didn't do this, the Lord did it. President Hinckley pointed out why the Lord did this in an address commemorating the restoration of the priesthood:

> The Lord of Heaven organized His priesthood into quorums. These are superior to any organization created by men. They come of the genius of God. We are so organized to *support and sustain one another,* to *build and strengthen one another,* to *multiply*

our individual capacities in service to others, and to coordinate our individual strengths to move forward the kingdom of God in the earth. ("Priesthood Perspectives," *Ensign,* February 1999, 72; emphasis added)

If someone asks you why the Lord organized his priesthood into quorums, would you be able to answer the question? If you can't, reread the statement by President Hinckley; you'll find four reasons that we have quorums. You are going to be in a quorum your whole Church life, so it becomes important to understand the purposes of being in a quorum.

The Aaronic Priesthood is organized into three quorums. When you are ordained a deacon, you become a member of the deacons quorum. The deacons quorum, according to the Lord's instruction, consists of twelve deacons with a presidency called by the bishop from among the deacons. The bishop, your Aaronic Priesthood leaders, and your quorum presidency help you understand your duties and opportunities for receiving special blessings in your life, and how you fit into the quorum (see D&C 107:85).

When you are ordained a teacher, you automatically become a member of the teachers quorum (see D&C 107:86). And the same holds true when you are ordained a priest (see D&C 107:87). In the priests quorum, however, your bishop serves as the president and selects counselors from among the members of the priests quorum.

Belonging to a quorum is a sacred privilege that comes when you receive the priesthood. The benefits of becoming a part of your quorum are phenomenal. You have an opportunity to learn with other young men your age, develop unique friendships among these young men, seek their help, give your help when it is needed, and feel a strong sense of brotherhood and unity.

Elder Boyd K. Packer said, "One can become careless with his quorum membership. Just as membership in a family or patriotism toward one's country may weaken and fail, so may quorum membership if it is taken for granted. In our day there is an urgent need for every single holder of the priesthood to bolster his spiritual patriotism or allegiance to his quorum" (*The Priesthood* [Salt Lake City: Deseret Book, 1981], 92).

What can you do as a quorum member to strengthen your quorum and yourself? Let's consider a few ideas:

1. Attend your quorum meetings and listen carefully to what leaders and quorum advisors say. Attending your meetings for the first few times may feel a little scary at first, much like going into a new grade in school. Keep in mind that you probably know most of the young men and should fit in rather quickly.

2. Participate in quorum activities, even if you aren't interested in some of them. Suggest ideas for future activities. Accept and fulfill assignments. Do things the way you think the Lord would do them. You are his representative now and hold his priesthood authority.

3. Be worthy to perform all ordinances and duties associated with your office in the priesthood. As you prepare, bless, or pass the sacrament, be sure that you do nothing during the week that would make you feel uncomfortable or unworthy to administer the sacrament in memory of the great sacrifice that the Savior made for us.

When you were ordained a deacon, you may have had an experience similar to the one recounted by Elder Robert L. Backman in the October 1982 general conference. Elder Backman told the story of a newly called deacon named Mark E. Petersen. Shortly after his ordination as a deacon, Mark received a call from the deacons quorum presidency to schedule an appointment with him and his parents at their home.

Promptly at the hour set, the doorbell rang. The members of the presidency stood on the porch, dressed in suits, white shirts, and ties, and each one carrying his scriptures. Sitting down with Mark and his parents, they began with prayer, and then handed an agenda to everyone there. The president then opened the scriptures, having Mark and his father read those references which speak of the power of the Aaronic Priesthood, what it is, and the particular duties of a deacon. The president then spoke about Mark's particular responsibilities and duties: how he should dress, how he should pass the sacrament, act as a messenger, collect fast offerings. And then they asked him if he had any questions. At the end of the visit they welcomed him to the quorum and offered help whenever he needed it. As they left, Mark . . . said to his Dad: "They were awesome!" ("Revitalizing Aaronic Priesthood Quorums," *Ensign,* November 1982, 38).

If you didn't have an experience like this when you joined your deacons quorum, and think it might be worthwhile for the quorum presidency to welcome new members into the quorum in this fashion, suggest it to the presidency. If you become a member of the presidency, you will have additional opportunities to identify effective ways to welcome new members into your quorum.

Sometimes young men view the quorum as merely a class they attend on Sunday and miss the whole concept of belonging to a quorum. Let's conclude this chapter with an illuminating statement by Elder L. Lionel Kendrick of the Seventy:

> We hope that you young men will view your quorum as much more than a Sunday class. It is a team of young men committed to gospel principles, unified in the knowledge that Jesus is the Christ, worthy and willing to exercise their priesthood power, and dedicated to serving one another and others. You will be a member of a priesthood quorum all the rest of your life. Learn to value it as a cherished group of friends and colleagues where you are a member in good standing with the love, respect, admiration, and cooperation of every other member. Make your quorum the kind of experience that will last long into your lifetime and, wherever you serve in the Church, you will remember the experiences, examples, opportunities, and blessings you had as a young man in a deacons, teachers, or priests quorum. ("The Quorum," *New Era,* May 1993, 57)

Chapter 8

How to Carry Out the Duties of Your Office

No church operates with as widespread use of giving and using priesthood authority as does The Church of Jesus Christ of Latter-day Saints. Every young man is expected to receive this authority and work in various offices and callings. This is how the work of the Lord gets done. He is not present to do it himself, so he has called you to do it.

When you first receive the Aaronic Priesthood and are ordained a deacon, you mostly likely have only a basic understanding of how to use your newly acquired authority. You don't yet attend seminary, and unlike other religious organizations, we don't attend divinity school to learn various forms and offices. You will probably make a mistake now and then, or feel awkward when you first use your priesthood in performing a task. Don't worry about it. Every beginner makes mistakes and feels a little clumsy when trying something for the first time. Things will smooth out as you go along.

You will find that your greatest growth and joy comes as you inconvenience yourself and make even small sacrifices of time and effort. It is easy to participate in a party, but a little more effort is required to go out in the rain and collect fast offerings or visit a sick quorum member. However, the effort is worth it. Even the effort to get up in the morning and attend church regularly brings personal growth and joy.

The Lord has specifically stated that you are now a "standing minister" given authority by him to watch over his Church and minister to the needs of the Saints as directed by the bishop or branch president (see D&C 84:111). Can you even imagine that at twelve years of age, you are a *minister* clothed with the holy priesthood to represent and do the work of the Lord! You are truly no ordinary young man! Be grateful for your calling and happy for this extraordinary blessing in your life.

The quickest—and best—way to learn your duties as a deacon is to start performing them. You may be a little nervous at first, but when you perform your duties consistently and frequently, you will feel less anxious about how to do them and you will understand them better. In addition, you will please the Lord and he will reveal many gospel and priesthood insights to you through the gift of the Holy Ghost, which you were given when you were baptized.

As a deacon, some of your duties include passing the sacrament, visiting the homes of members collecting fast offerings, providing messenger service for the bishop and his counselors, home teaching when there are insufficient teachers and priests, assisting the bishop with temporal things, fellowshipping other quorum members and other young men, and watching over the Church as well as inviting all to come unto Christ.

You must conduct yourself properly in these priesthood

activities. Remember, you now represent the Lord as you fulfill your assignments in the Aaronic Priesthood. That means you should be neat and clean in appearance. When you represent the Lord, you must be warm and friendly, yet dignified. Some boyhood behaviors are not appropriate when doing the work of the Lord. For instance, you may have seen deacons joke, make funny faces, push each other around, and act in a light-minded manner when passing the sacrament or collecting fast offerings.

While you don't have to be deadly serious when you are serving the Lord, it is best to avoid behaviors that draw attention to yourself and away from the task at hand. When you pass the sacrament, remember the crucifixion of our Savior and his Atonement for us. Remember that you are helping ward members renew sacred covenants with the Lord. By keeping those covenants, ward members seek for the Holy Spirit to guide them. Passing the sacrament is a wonderful assignment and should be performed with deep feelings of reverence and respect.

When you collect fast offerings, remember that you are simply acting for the bishop and the Lord. You are gathering the offerings of the Saints so that those who are in need of assistance can be helped. A happy attitude, sincere smile, and warm handshake will go a long way in carrying out this assignment as a servant of the Lord.

Never in the history of the Church have deacons been content to simply hold quorum meetings. Always, deacons have been organized to carry out important assignments, including to warn, expound, exhort, teach, and invite all to come unto Christ. Sounds like a pretty big assignment, doesn't it? But you are ready for the challenge. You have something most people don't have—the authority to act in the Lord's name.

In addition, you have been given certain keys and powers that enable you to act with faith and confidence. As you warn, invite, and teach others, you help meet the spiritual needs of the members of the Church. When you are invited to speak in church or share your thoughts during a priesthood lesson, prayerfully prepare your talks and ideas so that the Holy Ghost will witness the truthfulness of your words. Always be prepared to share your testimony when mingling with friends, when home teaching, and when holding family home evening.

Because you now hold the Aaronic Priesthood and have the authority to act for God, you are different from the rest of the world. You are not better than anyone else, but you have the responsibility to live a better life than others; more is expected of you than of those who do not hold such priesthood keys and blessings.

Interestingly, you may find that when you serve someone, you are the one who seems to receive the greater reward. Even if you are asked to distribute a Christmas message from the bishop on the darkest and coldest of winter nights, you will feel warm spiritually and know that what you are doing is right. People who receive the Christmas message will be grateful, but you will leave the assignment with a stronger testimony and a feeling of confidence and well-being.

Through service, fellowshipping, and being friendly, you are actually the one who receives the greatest growth and blessings. You learn quickly that when you are given an assignment, you must carry it out and report your success to your leader. This pattern of behavior will serve you well your whole life, whether at school, home, church, or work. You'll acquire feelings of respect and compassion when you help those who need your help. You'll have feelings of holiness and reverence when you help administer the sacrament, and you'll experience deep feelings of admiration and respect when you follow your Church leaders and do what they ask of you.

The Lord's promise to you is that if you "magnify your calling" in the priesthood, He will pour out blessings upon you. He will lift you up when you feel weak, speak peace to your mind when you are confused, and give you guidance and impressions to help you navigate through the turbulence that you find coming into your life as you grow through your teenage years. Be a faithful deacon and the opportunity will come to you to become a teacher and priest and learn even more about the powers and blessings of the Aaronic Priesthood.

Chapter 9

Why Do What Your Quorum President Asks of You

We know a young man in a local high school who is a member of the teachers quorum in his ward. He is a talented athlete who is also an elected officer of his high school class and a winning baseball pitcher. At school, he is highly respected as he directs the affairs of the class and takes a leadership role on the baseball team. However, in his ward, he takes direction from his quorum president and respects and supports the president.

It is easy to fall prey to the misconception that popularity in school is more important than a calling in a priesthood quorum. Your priesthood quorum president should be given honor and respect far beyond that accorded to outstanding students in school.

As with any organization, the officially designated officers hold the authority to conduct its affairs and the responsibility to help its members achieve their highest goals. In Church organizations, every male who is ordained to the priesthood has the inherent authority to preside over and conduct meetings and activities of Church members. Without the priesthood, the Church could not exist. No official act in the Church can be performed without the priesthood.

There is a difference, however, between holding either priesthood—Aaronic or Melchizedek—and holding an administrative position in the priesthood. To hold an administrative priesthood position, a male member must first hold the priesthood. In addition, he must be called, sustained, and set apart. When this pattern is followed and a quorum president is called, it means that the quorum president is officially designated as the person with the authority to direct the affairs of the quorum.

The president of a deacons quorum or a teachers quorum has no more priesthood than any other member of the quorum, but he holds the power to direct the official labors performed in the quorum by quorum members. Thus, an officially called, sustained, and set-apart quorum president is the person who holds the keys to the administration of the quorum; he is qualified to receive your attention, respect, and obedience.

The quorum president and his counselors are responsible for teaching you your priesthood duties and for giving you assignments that allow you to learn how to perform those duties. The phrase *to magnify your calling* means that you accept quorum assignments and serve others to increase your understanding of the gospel and enjoy the blessings of membership in the quorum. Quorum meetings are held regularly to help quorum members magnify their callings by planning ways to meet the needs of quorum members, to learn about the gospel and priesthood opportunities, and to build unity among quorum members by sharing testimonies and cultivating friendships.

The quorum president is obligated to take the lead in

teaching quorum members, in giving assignments, in cultivating friendships, in sharing testimonies, and in strengthening unity among quorum members. On the other hand, quorum members are equally obligated to learn about the gospel, to accept assignments, to share testimonies, to build true friendships, and bring about unity in the quorum. This all begins with respect for the quorum president and his counselors and your willingness to accept their leadership.

The authority of a quorum president must be exercised in a manner that benefits the members of the quorum. The Lord has said that "we have learned by sad experience that it is the nature and disposition of almost all men, as soon as they get a little authority, as they suppose, they will immediately begin to exercise unrighteous dominion. Hence many are called, but few are chosen" (D&C 121:39–40).

Then we are informed that "no power or influence can or ought to be maintained by virtue of the priesthood, only by persuasion, by long-suffering, by gentleness and meekness, and by love unfeigned" (D&C 121:39–41). This admonition drives right to the heart of priesthood leadership, to instruct and urge others to believe in and act in accord with gospel principles by persuasion and kindness, with gentleness and meekness, and with increased love for each member of the quorum (see D&C 121:42–46).

John A. Widtsoe, a deceased member of the Twelve Apostles and president of two universities—Utah State University and the University of Utah—advises that "the moment a man in a subordinate position begins to usurp the authority of his leader, that moment he is out of his place, and proves by his conduct that he does not comprehend his duty, [then] . . . he is not acting in the line of his calling, and is a dangerous character" (*Priesthood and Church Government* [Salt Lake City: Deseret Book, 1939], 195). Elder Widtsoe further explains that dangerous characters fall into error, set bad examples, and mislead others. This is not the kind of example you want to set for others. As one who holds the Aaronic Priesthood, your goal should be to honor, respect, and obey your priesthood leader.

You may feel a little like the nonmember whom Elder Gene Cook took to hear one of the General Authorities speak. After the meeting, the man observed, "Well, he is nothing but *a man.*"

Elder Cook responded by saying, "I suppose that he expected to see an angel, a demonstration of the gift of tongues, or something like that as a physical evidence of the General Authority's divine call." Elder Cook then makes our point: "Where do you stand on this important matter of spiritually seeing your leaders the way the Lord sees them? Our response to that question ought to be like the faithful Israelites' response to Joshua: 'And they answered Joshua, saying, All that thou commandest us we will do, and whithersoever thou sendest us, we will go'" (Joshua 1:16–17).

Elder Cook continues, "Remember, last of all, we do not desire blind obedience in the Church. We desire that every individual may know for himself that the counsel he receives from his leaders comes from the Lord. He has the right and the great privilege to know for himself of the Lord that he has been counseled aright. If he will be patient and wait upon the Lord, he will find that his priesthood leaders truly do counsel in righteousness, thus enabling him to walk upon safe ground ("Seek Out Your Spiritual Leader," *Ensign,* May 1978, 64–66).

You have priesthood leaders whom you should respect and from whom you take direction and counsel. That is the Lord's way and that is the way to treat your quorum president.

Part II

Adding Significant Power to the Aaronic Priesthood

Chapter 10

Something You Should Know about the Power of the Priesthood

The power of the priesthood can be compared with several different types of powers. Have you ever wondered how many kilowatts are in an average bolt of lightning? Scientists estimate, roughly, that there may be as many as 1 trillion. At three cents a kilowatt, such a bolt is worth $30 million. Would a power company jump at the chance to harness the electricity in a single bolt of lightning? You bet!

What is the power of an electrical storm? Is that just wasted energy? In fact, it isn't. Average lightning storms produce about 40 million tons of nitrogen each year, which is then spread over the earth by rain, keeping the earth green and verdant. At a price of $100 per ton, the nitrogen would be worth $4 billion. Who controls lightning storms? God controls them through the power of the priesthood.

By contrast, how puny are the powers of people to control and investigate the universe! Billions of dollars have been spent to put rocket ships into space and on the moon, a celestial body so close to the earth that it practically touches it, in the scheme of distances in the universe. A rocket used to propel a capsule into space is an awesome sight when ignited, but it is lighter in total weight than a large rock lying on a mountainside. Compared to the countless worlds Jesus has placed in orbit with the priesthood and holds in place with perfect control, our space effort is insignificant.

The full power of the priesthood of God is incomprehensible to our finite minds. There is no other power like it—adequate to create and control planets, yet so gentle that it can heal the tender tissues in the body of a small infant.

The power of the priesthood has been the enabling force to dot the world with chapels and tabernacles, and make Temple Square one of the most inspirational tourist attractions in the world. How important is the priesthood in our daily lives? The priesthood operates in every aspect of our lives, as electricity does. It is as close as every breath we draw. The priesthood power placed atmosphere on our earth, making it possible for us to live on its surface.

Once you understand the authority of the priesthood in general, you must then develop the power of the Aaronic Priesthood specifically. The Lord says that the powers of heaven cannot be controlled or handled except through principles of righteousness (see D&C 121:36). When you were given the Aaronic Priesthood, you were given the authority to act for the Lord. To act with faith, confidence, and the guidance of the Spirit and unleash the powers of heaven, you need to make every effort to increase your righteousness. Power depends on personal righteousness and the pattern of your life.

Bishop H. Burke Peterson, former first counselor in the Presiding Bishopric said:

> There is a difference between priesthood authority and priesthood power. Power and authority in the priesthood are not necessarily synonymous. All of us who hold the priesthood have the authority to act for the Lord, but the effectiveness of our authority—or if you please, the power that comes through that authority—depends on the pattern of our lives; it depends on our righteousness. Note again, "The powers of heaven cannot be controlled nor handled only upon principles of righteousness." ("Priesthood Authority and Power," *Ensign,* May 1976, 32)

In the next few chapters of this book, we will focus on ways to increase your righteousness and develop your priesthood power. As you examine each way, think about how you might use each idea to bring about a transformation in your life so that you will have priesthood power rather than only priesthood authority. Having authority is good, but exercising authority with power from the heavens is better.

We can't stress too much the importance of applying these ideas to your own life, to make them part and parcel of who you are and what you stand for. You must be strong in order to pursue this goal. You can't be weak and expect to overcome the barriers that may be put in your path. You must have a dogged determination to succeed. Only in this way will you actually acquire the power of the priesthood.

The ideas in these next chapters range widely, encompassing such actions as kneeling in prayer, studying the scriptures, and fasting regularly, as well as talking with your parents, bearing your testimony, attending seminary, and doing the right thing at school and in the community.

As has been said in the scriptures many times, as a result of doing what is required to develop power in the priesthood, you will be known for your works. You will become a different person. You will be as a beacon on a hill. You will acquire the strength to endure. As prophets of old, you will have the reputation as a man of power and integrity. You will be honored along with our pioneer forefathers as stalwart and strong. No greater gift can be given to your parents and to your descendants than being a man with power in the priesthood.

Before you start the next chapter, let's read again from the Doctrine and Covenants, starting with section 121, verse 3. "Behold, there are many called, but few are chosen. And why are they not chosen? Because their hearts are set so much upon the things of this world, and aspire to the honors of men, that they do not learn this one lesson—that the rights of the priesthood are inseparably connected with the powers of heaven, and that the powers of heaven cannot be controlled nor handled only upon the principles of righteousness."

You have been called and given authority to act for the Lord. Do not put the things of the world or the honors of men first. Rather, "seek ye first the kingdom of God and his righteousness; and all these things shall be added unto you" (see Matthew 6:33).

This is the Lord's promise to you. The Lord always keeps his promises. Do not falter. Put the goal of increased righteousness first, and you will open up the marvelous powers of heaven. The Lord will also "add to you" and help you with other needs and opportunities so that you can succeed in the world in which you live.

Chapter 11

Study the Scriptures

Early in this dispensation of the restored gospel, the Lord spoke of the early elders of the Church, saying, "And whatsoever they shall speak when moved upon by the Holy Ghost shall be scripture, shall be the will of the Lord" (D&C 68:4).

Scriptures are divine directions from the Lord. Here is a question for you: Are you studying these divine directions on a daily basis? The scriptures have been likened to a road map. They provide directions for finding our way through life. When we fail to read, study, and ponder the scriptures, we may find ourselves going backwards on the path that is supposed to be leading to eternal life!

When the new editions of the standard works with their valuable study helps were completed, President Hinckley said:

> I have read these great and singular volumes again and again.
>
> As I have pondered their words there has come, by the power of the Holy Ghost, a witness of their truth and divinity.
>
> I do not concern myself much with reading long commentary volumes designed to enlarge at length upon that which is found in the scriptures. Rather, I prefer to dwell with the source, taste of the unadulterated waters of the fountain of truth—the word of God as he gave it and as it has been recorded in the books we accept as scripture.
>
> Where there are questions, or where cross-referencing will help, the tools in the new editions will be invaluable. Through reading the scriptures, we can gain the assurance of the Spirit that that which we read has come of God for the enlightenment, blessing, and joy of his children.
>
> I urge our people everywhere to read the scriptures more—to study all of them together with the help of these tremendous aids for a harmony of understanding in order to bring their precepts into our lives.
>
> May the Lord bless each of us to feast upon his holy word and to draw from it that strength, that peace, that knowledge "which passeth all understanding" (Philippians 4:7), as he has promised. ("Feasting upon the Scriptures," *Ensign*, December 1985, 42)

For many Church members, reading the scriptures is the quickest way to feel the Spirit of the Lord and to receive the reassurance that everything will work out for their best good—especially when they are feeling discouraged or confused.

Start now, if you haven't already, to read the scriptures regularly. Find a time that is best for you. Be committed to read for a few minutes every day. Keep a pencil with you, so that you can mark certain passages or write in the margins any ideas or observations that impress you. If you can, share an important concept or insight that you have learned with someone else, thereby helping them learn and helping you remember. Try to feel the Spirit of the Lord. You will be amazed at the testimony of truth and the peace that comes to you as you regularly read and ponder the scriptures.

Before we came to dwell on this earth, we received much instruction, divine direction, love, and support from our Heavenly Father. But how do we keep informed so that we are properly prepared to thrive while here on earth and then return home with honor to our Heavenly Father?

President Harold B. Lee quoted President Brigham Young and said a stunning thing about returning to Heavenly Father:

> If any of us could see the God we are striving to serve, if we could see our Father who dwells in the heavens, we should learn that we are as well acquainted with him as we are with our earthly father; and he would be as familiar to us in the expression of his countenance and we should be ready to embrace him, if we had the privilege. We know much about God if we but realized it, and there is no other item that will so much astound you, when your eyes are opened in eternity, as to think that you were so stupid in the body. (*Stand Ye in Holy Places* [Salt Lake City: Deseret Book, 1975], 27–28)

To return home to Heavenly Father and to avoid being "stupid in the body," we need to continue to receive directions and instructions from our Heavenly Father. These instructions come to us personally and through the voice of the Lord's chosen prophets, seers, and revelators. When they come through the Lord's chosen servants, they are called *scripture*.

Do you remember the elements of Lehi's dream? You may

recall the straight and narrow path that led to the tree of life, which Lehi urged his family to follow. The difficulty in traveling the narrow path came about because of a river of filthy water on one side and a tower of pride on the other. Then, to make matters even more difficult, a dark mist arose, obscuring the path. The only safe way to reach the tree of life was to hold on to the iron rod, or in other words, the word of God (1 Nephi 8).

The word of God is (1) contained in the scriptures; (2) contained in the directions given by the living prophet and those whom we sustain as prophets, seers, and revelators; and (3) in the inspiration we receive from the Spirit of the Lord. When you read the scriptures, seek for the inspiration of the Lord concerning how what you read can be applied in your own life. When you listen to the prophet and the Lord's servants, you receive not only direction from their words but also inspiration from the Lord to know the most important thing for you to do right now.

Heavenly Father gave you marvelous instructions before you were born into this earth life. He wants to continue giving you directions for your guidance in returning safely to him. He gives that guidance through the scriptures, words of the prophet, and personal inspiration. You will be amazed at how much better you feel simply by reading the scriptures ten minutes each day.

It's now up to you as a priesthood holder to take advantage of this wonderful opportunity and to feel the strength and encouragement of the words of the Lord in your daily life. There is no question but that reading and pondering the scriptures regularly will increase your personal righteousness and increase your priesthood power. Without these divine scriptural directions, any of us could actually end up more stupid in the body than we ever thought possible!

Chapter 12

Kneel in Prayer, Morning and Night

Elder Russell M. Nelson of the Quorum of the Twelve Apostles pointed out an important reason for praying during a recent conference address. Elder Nelson explained that he was visiting a nursing care facility, and during that visit, he spoke with a woman about her family. She had three sons and told him about her two sons who visited her regularly. When asked about the third son, she answered with tears in her eyes, "I haven't heard from him for years. I don't even know how many grandchildren I have."

Elder Nelson then said, "If such a mother yearns to hear from her sons, it is easy to see why a loving Father in Heaven wants to hear from His children. Through prayer, we can show our love for God. He has made it so easy. We may pray to Him any time. No special equipment is needed. We don't even need to charge batteries or pay a monthly service fee" ("Sweet Power of Prayer," *Ensign,* May 2003, 7).

God loves you. He is your Heavenly Father. He wants to hear from you and help you. Aaronic Priesthood holders like yourself, who have authority to represent him in important assignments, should be good examples to everyone they meet. You have a special need to follow the advice of Alma: "Counsel with the Lord in *all* thy doings, and he will direct thee for good; yea, when thou liest down at night lie down unto the Lord, that he may watch over you in your sleep; and when thou risest in the morning let thy heart be full of thanks unto God" (Alma 37:37). You know from the scriptures and the examples given that you should pray often. You also know that Heavenly Father *wants to hear from you and help you.*

You should pray at least twice a day. Why is that? You should pray in the morning because your daily activities have a strong tendency to distract you from your spiritual goals and take your mind off of your spiritual needs. You need the assurance and assistance of your Heavenly Father so that you will do your best throughout the day.

Then you need to pray in the evening to get back in touch with your Heavenly Father.

After a long day of trying to stay on the straight and narrow path, and negotiate the problems and difficulties of living in a complex world, you need to reconnect with your Father in Heaven. You need to thank him for allowing you to survive the day and resist temptation to do wrong. Temptations will confront you all day long. One prayer is not enough to help you resist doing wrong. You must pray more than once a day.

Why should you kneel in prayer? Kneeling is the ultimate form of reverence, showing deep respect for someone. When you address your Heavenly Father, and you want to use the deepest form of reverence, you should kneel in prayer. Showing deep reverence at least twice a day is a positive way to demonstrate sincere prayer.

You'll find several significant reasons for praying morning and night—and even throughout the day. There is little question that through prayer, you can find direction when you are confused, solutions when you have problems, strength when you feel weak, and peace when you seem almost overcome with the troubles that abound in the world around you.

We have been taught to pray since we were young children. Do you remember your mother or father or Primary teacher teaching you to be reverent, fold your arms, bow your head, and close your eyes when you pray?

Jesus told the Nephites "to pray always lest ye enter into temptation; for Satan desireth to have you, that he may sift you as wheat" (3 Nephi 18:18).

In our time, the Lord said to the Prophet Joseph Smith, "Pray always that you may come off conqueror" (D&C 10:5), and "Pray always lest that wicked one have power in you, and remove you out of your place" (D&C 93:49). This means that prayer will aid you to be more successful and avoid the temptations of Satan in your daily life. Prayer can create a barrier against engaging in evil acts. With regular prayer, you can receive direction from Heavenly Father, so that you won't succumb to the evil intentions of others.

Stop for a minute and think about your prayers. When you bless the food, do you rush through a short prayer similar to the one you offer each time you are asked to bless the food? Or, do you really feel filled with the spirit of thanksgiving for having good food to eat? When you pray in public, do you pay more attention to the audience listening to you than to Heavenly Father, to whom you are speaking? When you are praying quietly in the evening, do you find your mind wandering and losing focus on the purpose of your prayer?

Many young people, and quite a number of older people, encounter various problems when praying. Most prominent among these problems is being overly repetitious, letting your mind wander, sleepiness, feeling unworthy, praying in generalities instead of specifics, and sometimes not recognizing a need for guidance, especially when you are using your priesthood authority to do the Lord's work.

You have already learned that simply because you start out with "Father in Heaven" and end with "amen" doesn't mean that you have said an effective prayer. You are not a child anymore. You are a teenager with special authority from God to act in his name. As such you must make your prayers as effective as possible. Here are two powerful suggestions.

Don't Rush through Your Prayers

Take time to realize that you are about to talk to your Heavenly Father. Imagine that God is concerned about you, loves you, and wants to help you. Feel that He is very near and will listen to you. Pause briefly before you start and prepare yourself to engage in a great spiritual experience. Be determined that you are going to make very best use of your prayer time with your Heavenly Father. Proceed slowly and reverently. Try to block out all the turmoil and clatter of the world around you. Focus on the presence of your Father in Heaven.

Some people imagine that they are actually entering into the presence of Heavenly Father when they pray. They feel grateful to God for listening to them, helping them, and giving them the peace of mind and confidence to move forward in their lives and in serving him. They try to feel his presence and are prepared to thank him for their many blessings. They feel humbled to be engaged in praying to God and receiving insight and direction.

Avoid Mechanical Repetitions of Words and Phrases

Think specifically about what has happened in your life recently and what you are thankful for. For example, pray for assistance on a specific test that you're going to take, or pray for the recovery from an illness of a specific person.

Speak to Heavenly Father as a son would speak to his own loving father, heart to heart, realizing that Heavenly Father knows you through and through. You wouldn't talk to your earthly father in generalities; you would ask him for specific things. If something good happened to you during the day, you would tell your dad that you are thankful for that precise thing. When you speak with others, you are most likely yourself, open and be honest. Be this same way with your Father in Heaven. By being specific, you automatically avoid repetitious phrases and trite words.

Open your heart to him about your need for help as you fulfill priesthood assignments. Talk as though you were face to face with Him, and ask for His help as you try to fulfill your priesthood assignments and overcome the various temptations that come to young men. Take your time. These are some of the most precious and useful moments in your whole life.

When you are finished talking with your Father in Heaven, end with amen, but continue to hold the feeling in your heart that God loves you. Hold in your mind the thought that God is close to you and through his great power you are never alone.

When you end your prayer, depart with a feeling of confidence and assurance that, with the assistance of God, you can accomplish anything, if it is right for all involved.

Let's conclude our discussion on developing priesthood power through more effective praying by paraphrasing the Apostle Paul as he gives this powerful insight about prayer to the Saints at Philippi:

"Rejoice in the Lord always. Rejoice in everything by prayer and supplication with thanksgiving. Let your requests be made known unto God. And the peace of God, which passeth all understanding, shall be in your hearts and minds through Christ Jesus" (Philippians 4:4–7).

Chapter 13

Be Sensitive to Personal Inspiration

If you think of prayer as the way we communicate with God, and of inspiration as the main way that God communicates with us, then it all sounds quite simple. Elder Boyd K. Packer pointed out one problem, however:

> We succeed in the Church, by and large, in teaching our members to pray. Even our little ones are taught to fold their arms and bow their heads, and with whispered coaching from their parents, and from brothers and sisters, they soon learn how to pray.

There is one part of prayer—the answer part—
that perhaps, by comparison, we neglect. There are
some things about answers to prayer that you can
learn when you are very young, and they will be a
great protection to you.

Answers to prayers come in a quiet way. The
scriptures describe that voice of inspiration as a
still, small voice. If you really try, you can learn
to respond to that voice. ("Prayers and Answers,"
Ensign, November 1979, 19)

You may have already received personal inspiration but didn't
recognize it. Think of a moment when you were relaxed, away
from the confusion and noise that so often surrounds us. Perhaps
you were reading the scriptures and felt a surge of joy and truth
course through you that let you know that what you were reading
was in fact true. Or maybe you were listening to the prophet
speak at general conference, and as he spoke, you were brought
to a state of knowing and understanding that what he was saying
was true. Maybe you even experienced a flash of insight as you
recalled something that you should change in your own life. Or
perhaps you heard a priesthood leader or Sunday School teacher
describe an experience in his or her life. You felt the truthfulness
of it and received an impression that you should be more sensitive
to a similar issue in your own life. These impressions come from
the Spirit and are right and true. They give us great comfort as
well as guidance.

Many years ago, Elder Melvin J. Ballard, the grandfather of
our present-day apostle Elder M. Russell Ballard, made a powerful
statement at the conclusion of a Sunday School conference in the
Salt Lake Tabernacle. He called the gift of the Holy Ghost "the
most precious of man's possessions while he dwells in mortality.
Let us stir up that gift that it may be profitable to us in the
solution of the problems of today, I pray, in the name of Jesus
Christ, Amen" ("Discourses on the Holy Ghost," *The Instructor,*
June 1933, 244).

Let's emphasize two main points that are essential to you

as a young priesthood holder trying to develop power in the priesthood. The first point that Elder Melvin Ballard makes is that the gift of the Holy Ghost "is the most precious of man's possessions while he dwells in mortality." That means that while we are away from our Heavenly Father and dwelling here on this earth without even a clear memory of where we came from, the Holy Ghost can be our companion so that we never have to feel alone. If we live worthy of his companionship, He will help us through all of the daily challenges that we have in life. He will give us guidance and protection as well as peace of mind and comfort.

The second point made by Elder Ballard is that we must "stir up" the gift of the Holy Ghost so that it will be helpful in solving our daily problems. Think of it. You have the third member of the Godhead to help you solve problems and make excellent personal decisions. Who wouldn't want to live a worthy life and have the companionship and help of the Holy Ghost in getting through the problems and temptations that come on almost an hourly basis?

As we seek direction in our lives and answers to our prayers, we receive promptings that should be clear and unmistakable. Listen to the testimony of President Hinckley concerning inspiration:

> Keep yourselves open to the inspiration of the Lord. Listen to the whisperings of the Spirit. I remember when Brother Harold B. Lee set me apart as a stake president. He said, "Listen for the whisperings of the Spirit in the stillness of the night." Now I believe in that. I have seen in my experience, and I think I can testify that the Lord has spoken quietly. I didn't hear any words, but in the middle of the night ideas have come into my head which, I think, have been prophetic in their nature" (Devotional, Provo Missionary Training Center, 26 June 1998).

If you are distracted by the noise and confusion around you, it becomes more difficult to hear the still, quiet voice of the Spirit. Inappropriate music, breaking the Word of Wisdom, conduct unbecoming to a priesthood holder, and unruly behavior all tend to offend the Spirit of the Lord and hinder the reception of impressions and promptings.

Elder Richard G. Scott of the Quorum of the Twelve Apostles adds this important comment with regard to receiving personal inspiration:

> A communication to the heart is a more general impression. The Lord often begins by giving impressions. Where there is recognition of their importance and they are obeyed, one gains more capacity to receive more detailed instruction to the mind. An impression to the heart, if followed, is fortified by a more specific instruction to the mind. Enos, whose soul hungered, kneeled down immediately before God and cried unto him in mighty prayer. Soon hereafter the voice of the Lord came into Enos's mind and spoke specific thoughts to him. ("Helping Others to Be Spiritually Led," General Authority Address, The Twenty-Second Annual Church Educational System Religious Educators Symposium, Brigham Young University, 11 August 1998, 4)

Nothing is more exciting than getting up in the morning and asking our Heavenly Father to bless us with ideas and inspiration throughout the day so that we can see opportunities to help ourselves and others overcome problems and challenges. You will be wonderfully surprised at the ideas that come to your mind about schoolwork, ways to succeed at achieving a goal, how to get along better with someone, doing a better job in your priesthood assignments, and on and on and on.

If you are trying to live a righteous life and keep the commandments, you should expect to receive and recognize personal inspiration. Being inspired is one of the most exciting things that can happen each day of your life. And receiving inspiration will strengthen your faith and testimony that Heavenly Father is continually trying to help you through the inspiration of the Spirit.

Your challenge is threefold: 1) be sensitive enough to recognize impressions as they come to you, 2) write impressions down so you won't forget them, and 3) act upon impressions as quickly as possible. When the Lord sees that you are listening to and obeying the promptings of the Spirit, he will give you more impressions.

In fact, that is exactly how you grow in the spirit of personal revelation and inspiration. Receiving and obeying impressions from the Spirit of the Lord adds to your confidence in school, at home, and in your daily life. Receiving personal inspiration also increases your power when you are exercising the authority of the Aaronic Priesthood.

Chapter 14

Talk Frequently with Your Mom and Dad

Chris Crow recounts the story of a teenage boy who stayed out past curfew to talk with a friend whose parents were getting a divorce. By the time the boy got home, he was an hour past the deadline. When he finally rushed home, he found the porch light on, so he tiptoed in the front door only to find an outraged dad, ready to confront him about being late.

The boy tried to explain that he was helping a friend, but his father dismissed those efforts with the conclusion that his son was late and that was that—the boy was grounded. The boy was worried about his friend and frustrated in his attempts to talk with his dad, who only wanted to argue with him about being late. The young man wished that things could be different (see "How to Talk to you Parents," *New Era,* February 1989, 14).

Generally speaking, parents and children have always had different points of view on certain issues. In the above example, the young man thought that helping a friend took priority over curfew for being home. This situation was an ideal opportunity for the boy and his father to spend a little time talking to each other, listening to each other, and strengthening their relationship with each other.

Maybe you've had a similar experience with your parents. Everyone knows that kids and parents disagree. Parents want their children to obey them, and when they appear to deliberately ignore their instructions, parents may be shocked. As a young priesthood holder, sit down and talk over your differences with your parents. Sometimes you can disagree with your parents but in an agreeable way!

This whole business of talking frequently with your mom and dad is serious stuff. Experts who have studied communication say that communication is the primary vehicle of all human interaction. That means that the most important way we interact and relate to each other is by talking. Communication experts also observe that when you talk to your parents in a polite and honest way, your relationship with them is better.

As a priesthood holder, you already know that you should "honor thy father and thy mother: that thy days may be long upon the land which the Lord thy God giveth thee" (Exodus 20:12).

Honor means to show respect and care. One of the simplest ways you can show respect and care to your parents is to talk to them. They want to know how you are doing at school and with your friends. Talk to them and tell them. This shows that you respect them and care about enlightening them instead of leaving them in the dark about how you are doing. One of the most common ways to disrespect your parents is to ignore them, isolate yourself from them, and not talk to them.

Your parents have spent years trying to teach you what is

right and what is wrong. They are a tremendous resource for you and can guide you and help you with any problem or concern that comes up in your life. Since they know you better than anyone else on the face of the earth, don't quit talking to them because you think you may know more than they do about your challenges in life.

Sometimes your parents may seem too busy to stop what they're doing to listen to you. Sometimes they may seem tired or distracted with a problem of their own. Occasionally, parents are so occupied keeping everything in the family headed in the right direction that they fail to give you an opportunity to speak privately to them. Your job is to be patient and persistent until you find a moment of calm when you can talk to your mom and dad.

Although you may feel that your parents may sometimes feel too busy to talk, you may discover that you are the one who is too busy. Maybe you need to examine your own plans to see if you can reduce or even eliminate some of your "busyness" and give your parents a sign that you genuinely do want to talk with them.

This talking and listening is not namby-pamby stuff—it is the substance of good relationships. Tough guys can listen as well as anyone, especially if they want to build a strong family and avoid the constant complaining and quibbling that occurs when people are under too much stress.

You may possibly have to be somewhat direct to get past communication barriers that exist between you and your parents. You could calmly say, "Dad, I've got something I want to tell you, but you've got to listen to what I say without talking. When I'm finished, you can talk and I'll listen."

Your Dad might say surprise you and readily agree, or he might agree, but then concentrate on trying to defend himself and not really hear what you are saying. If that happens, you may have to persist in a calm and gentle manner until he actually hears, understands, and comprehends what you're talking about.

Overall, parents are not such bad people; they just sometimes think they're always right. Since they're older than you, they do have more experience than you do. But that is the very reason you want to respect them and talk to them frequently. You will find yourself enjoying significant benefits when you keep the channels of communication open between you and your mom and dad. Don't underestimate the value of your parents' experience. Just because you've lived for thirteen or sixteen years doesn't mean that you have adequate experience in all areas of life.

By way of summary, try to improve your communication with your parents by following these suggestions:

- Understand and believe that no matter what your parents say to you, they have your best interests in mind because they love you. They want you to be safe and, eventually, as happy as you can be. Regardless of what kinds of difficulties you might experience in trying to establish a warm and accepting communicative climate, do not give up.

- Talk to your mom and dad as frequently as you possibly can. By doing so, you honor them and build a trusting relationship with them. And, of course, you give them the opportunity to do what they want to do most, which is help and support you in achieving your goals and solving your problems.

- Listen to your parents. Give them a fair hearing and then ask them to listen to you. Be sure to give them time to think over your point of view. Don't press them for an immediate decision on important issues.

- Always keep your discussions calm and in control. Don't try to have a productive discussion when you are angry or upset.

- Keep things in perspective. Regardless of the number of differences you may have with your parents, focus on how much you agree upon. You love each other. You have had many good experiences together. You have created wonderful memories, made incredible sacrifices, love the gospel, and share many ideals and beliefs. If you think about it, you probably agree with your parents on ninety-nine out of every one hundred issues. Don't blow differences out of proportion and let them interfere with your relationship to your parents.

Believe it or not, your parents are your best friends. Keep working to create a positive relationship with your parents so that they can help you cope with the host of concerns you're bound to confront as you move through life.

Chapter 15

Why Practice
the Word of Wisdom?

A young missionary and his companion were teaching the gospel to a family in Florida. After several excellent discussions, the wife agreed to be baptized. The husband, however, couldn't give up smoking cigarettes. He was a friendly man and always greeted the missionaries with a hard slap on the back, or, when they were sitting, a hard slap to the leg. One missionary noticed that when they left the home, they often left with what looked like bruised blood vessels and a deep red spot where they had been slapped.

Finally, after several visits, the missionaries asked him what it would take to have him give up cigarettes and agree to baptism.

This strong man gave the elders an interesting challenge. "If you can do fifteen push-ups in the manner I describe," he said, "I will make a serious attempt to give up my cigarette-smoking habit. You must do a push up, get up and touch the wall, then do two push-ups, get up and touch the wall, and continue in that manner until you do fifteen push-ups." A quick calculation shows that the man was challenging the missionary to actually do one hundred twenty push-ups!

The missionary accepted the challenge. He had been keeping the Word of Wisdom but not practicing push-ups. The first sixty push-ups weren't too bad, but he began to tire. When he reached the fourteenth set, or one hundred and five total push-ups, his hands and arms shook, and he fell flat on his face. An inner urging said, "Get up, you can do it." Wearily the missionary stood up, touched the wall, and got down on the floor to attempt the final fifteen push-ups. He pleaded with the Lord, "If I ever needed a blessing, I need it now."

The missionary completed the final set of push-ups with less effort than some of the previous push-ups, much to the astonishment of the husband. The challenge had come unexpectedly, but with the help of the Lord, the challenge had been met successfully.

Here is what Dr. John A. Widtsoe, a scientist and former member of the Quorum of the Twelve, had to say about keeping the Word of Wisdom so that we can magnify our callings:

> Here, young men of Zion, is a subject worthy of our most serious thought and effort. We are preparing the way for the coming of Jesus Christ. Shall he come and find us with no attempt made toward physical uplifting and purification of our bodies? Will he come under such conditions? Shall we, the people with the most important mission of any people now on earth, permit our bodies, from a lack of information, to be weakened so that we cannot magnify our glorious missions? Think of it! One little error in diet may be committed at each meal! Three meals are eaten a day; there are three

hundred and sixty-five days in a year; the error is repeated more than one thousand times each year. No system can withstand such incessantly repeated attacks upon its health. Is it a wonder that men die young; or that age is full of weakness and pain? ("The Food of Man," *Improvement Era*, August 1901, 769–73)

Earlier, President Joseph F. Smith told us what happens when we break the Word of Wisdom. "Why is it that we are so dull and languid? It is because we break the Word of Wisdom, disease preys upon our systems, our understandings are darkened, and we do not comprehend the things of God; the devil takes advantage of us, and we fall into temptation" ("Meaning of the Word of Wisdom," *Improvement Era*, August 1901, 943–49).

About three years after the organization of the Church, the Lord gave a revelation that seems to describe perfectly the time in which you are living: "Behold, verily, thus saith the Lord unto you: In consequence of evils and designs which do and will exist in the hearts of conspiring men in the last days, I have warned you, and forewarn you, by giving unto you this word of wisdom by revelation" (D&C 89:4.)

When this revelation was given, there was no multimedia blitz to enslave you in the use of habit-forming drugs by advertising so many products that are harmful to your body. Now you see advertisements all around you—not aimed at older people but aimed directly at young people. Try an experiment the next time you are watching a sport program: notice all the beer commercials and how enticing they are. These advertisements, urging you to use various forms of alcohol, tobacco, and hot drinks, such as tea and coffee, are put together by knowledgeable men and women who are conspiring to hook you on their products.

One of your greatest temptations as a young man is break the Word of Wisdom. In addition to the craftiness of advertisers, you may find other young men your age who dare you, call you a coward, and try to get you to violate the Lord's law of health. The nearer you are to growing into honorable manhood and making your own choices, the greater the pressure may be to break this commandment from the Lord. That's why the Lord said, "I have warned you and forewarn you."

Many habit-forming drugs and stimulants are not mentioned in the Word of Wisdom. You have to use your common sense and figure out some things for yourself. For example, if caffeine is a habit-forming and stimulating ingredient in coffee, which is not good for your health, and caffeine is put into various brands of soda pop, wouldn't you be wise to avoid soda pop with caffeine in it?

We have been talking about some of the injurious substances to keep out of your body. The basic principles and nutritious materials that need to be brought into the body are also spelled out rather clearly in the revelation know as the Word of Wisdom. If you read Doctrine and Covenants 89 thoroughly, you will see that its recommendations are perfectly consistent with what the most nutritious, recommended, and researched diets encourage us to eat.

Briefly, the Lord, who created us and knows us better than anyone, recommends that we eat vegetables, referred to as herbs, and every fruit in the season thereof. Remember the juicy taste of a crisp, ripe apple as it literally pops in your mouth when you bite it, or how delicious a melon is when it is ripe in the summertime! They are a far more delicious diet than chips and soda pop.

The Lord directs us, in addition, to eat grains like wheat, which are available in many good cereals and bread. Meat is to be eaten sparingly and to be prepared carefully. In the words of President Ezra Taft Benson, "In general, the more food we eat in its natural state and the less it is refined without additives, the healthier it will be for us" ("Do Not Despair," *Ensign,* November 1974, 66).

If you want to be as healthy as possible, read Doctrine and Covenants 88, especially verses 121 and 123–26, and take note of what the Lord says about proper sleep, pride, idleness, finding fault, prayer, and charity. Then, follow the Lord's advice. You shouldn't do less.

If you keep the Word of Wisdom as well as walking in obedience to the commandments, here is what the Lord promises will happen to you:

> And all saints who remember to keep and do these sayings, walking in obedience to the commandments, shall receive health in their navel and marrow to their bones; And shall find wisdom and great treasures of knowledge, even hidden treasures; and shall run and not be weary, and shall walk and not faint. And I, the Lord, give unto them a promise, that the destroying angel shall pass by them, as the children of Israel, and not slay them. Amen." (D&C 89:18–21)

You have to be alert and wise to grow into manhood without getting hooked into breaking the Word of Wisdom. Focus on stories like the one about the missionary shared at the beginning of this chapter and the added strength that came to him when keeping the commandments, including the Word of Wisdom. You are old enough and smart enough to be aware of how conspiring men tempt you through alluring and enticing advertisements. Don't keep viewing and dwelling on those advertisements. Don't even take a dare or experiment out of curiosity with breaking the Word of Wisdom. Confessions to bishops are littered with sorrowful people explaining, "I thought it couldn't happen to me."

But most of all, remember the great promise of the Lord, that if you keep his laws and commandments, you will find wisdom and great treasures of knowledge, even hidden treasures of wisdom. Those blessings are available right now. The Lord will not fail to keep his promises to you if you do as he says.

Chapter 16

How to Keep the Sabbath Day Holy

In our modern day, the Lord said in a revelation: "And that thou mayest more fully keep thyself unspotted from the world, thou shalt go to the house of prayer and offer up thy sacraments upon my holy day; For verily this is a day appointed unto you to rest from your labors, and to pay thy devotions unto the Most High" (D&C 59: 9–10).

Let's look at one point for a minute: You should keep the Sabbath day holy so that you may more fully keep yourself unspotted from the world. *Unspotted* means to be unstained, unblemished, unflawed, and unmarked. The Lord is saying that if you keep the Sabbath day holy and go to church on Sunday, you will be able to resist being misled by the world and caught up in inappropriate Sabbath day activities, as well as unsavory activities other days of the week.

Look around you! More stores are open to shoppers on Sundays than ever before. Movie houses are looking for larger Sunday audiences. Sporting events are proliferating on Sundays. Supermarkets do a thriving business on Sundays. Entertainment in every form imaginable seems to be trying to attract your attention and attendance on Sundays. Of course, all the doughnut shops, ice cream places, fast food businesses, and service stations with snacks and treats are just waiting for you to come for a visit on Sunday.

In a few places, Aaronic Priesthood holders have been known to slip out of church between meetings or stop at a convenience store after meetings to buy food, drinks, and snacks. These businesses stay open because customers buy things. Are you one of the customers who helps keep these businesses operating on Sundays? Remember, you hold the priesthood and are a fellow servant of the Lord. You are supposed to be setting a good example for your friends and, ultimately, for the whole world. Keeping out of businesses on Sunday is one way to do that.

Elder S. Dilworth Young worked with and loved the youth. He understood the challenges that you face, and he offered two good rules to follow with regard to keeping the Sabbath day holy:

"The first is to spend no money on Sunday. That will go a long way toward helping you to resist Sunday amusements.

The second is that you will wear your best clothes all day and not change into every-day wear. That will help, too" (*More Precious than Rubies* [Salt Lake City: Bookcraft, 1959], 99).

These are two brief but good rules for keeping yourself unsoiled and unspotted from enticements to break the Sabbath. If you don't spend money, you won't be able to buy anything. If you stay in your best clothes, you will be reminded that Sunday is a special day, a day to engage in the kind of activities that nourish and strengthen your spirit. You have six days to buy things and be entertained. You really don't need an additional day to do the same things.

Why keep the Sabbath day holy? The whole world of entertainment, recreation, and commercialism is going to fall right on top of your head on Sunday unless you do something about it. You may already have friends who are treating Sunday just like the other six days of the week. They lie around in bed until late in the morning and, when they finally get up and get going, they try to find some buddies with whom they can go play golf, go to a movie, or watch a sporting event.

You have to take a stand if you are going to avoid getting caught up in the onslaught of social and worldly activities that are surrounding you. The Lord knows everything, and he knew that you were going to find yourself in this exact situation with regard to keeping the Sabbath day holy.

The Lord's directions are powerful and clear, even a little blunt. If you want to extract yourself from some of the noise and clatter of the world on Sunday, and you want to keep the Sabbath day holy, minimally do these three things: go to church; rest from your labors and activities of the other six days; and do good things on the Sabbath (see D&C 59).

Obviously you can't go to church all day long, and you probably don't need to rest all day long. That brings you to the Lord's third directive: Do good things on the Sabbath. The Lord gets weary trying to spell out every detail of every commandment for us. This is where you must take responsibility for yourself and decide what good and holy things you can do on Sunday. Think about it, study it out in your mind, and then ask the Lord. He will tell you.

Once you have decided that the true purpose of the Sabbath is to keep yourself unspotted from the world, and you have asked the Lord for some direction, you might want to talk with your family about appropriate Sunday activities. You see, you are not alone in trying to figure out how to keep the Sabbath day holy. Your mother and father are facing the same challenges that you are, and they would probably like to talk about what kinds of activities are best suited for Sunday. Your brothers and sisters may also have excellent ideas about trying to keep the Sabbath day holy.

From all of the Lord's directions about keeping the Sabbath holy, you realize immediately that you and your family have interesting decisions to make about the amount of TV watching you do on Sunday. Of course, with the growing popularity of video games, you also have to make a decision about how many hours you are inspired to play video games on Sunday.

You have already learned that Sunday is a day of rest from the regular routine activities of work, study, and play that you engage in during the week. It is not a day to be lazy and turn into a couch potato. You may think that your activities are being severely restricted on Sundays, so you may tend to do very little of anything. If you follow the Lord's directions, you will quickly find out that your goal is to do *good* on the Sabbath, not to spend the day loafing around or trying to find a new form of recreation.

Realizing that fast Sunday sometimes doesn't pass very fast, and that the Sabbath lasts all day, not only until the end of church meetings, let's look at the kinds of things that might be appropriate to do on Sunday. Keep in mind, however, that the best approach to a useful, restful, and spiritual day is to follow the promptings of the Spirit.

Elder Charles Didier of the presidency of the Seventy, after reviewing both the Bible and modern scriptures, made a brief analysis of what is appropriate to do on the Sabbath day:

> As we review the Lord's pronouncements about the Sabbath in the Old Testament, the New Testament, the Book of Mormon, and the Doctrine and Covenants, we can learn some of the basic elements of Sabbath observance:
>
> 1. It is a day to rest from our labors.
> 2. It is a holy day of worship.
> 3. It is a day to remember the Lord's Atonement and resurrection.

4. It is a day to renew our baptismal covenants by partaking of the sacrament.

5. It is a day of prayer and fasting.

6. It is a day of listening to uplifting music, hymns, and songs.

7. It is a day to prepare, meditate, and study the gospel.

8. It is a day to visit the sick and the afflicted, the widows and orphans.

9. It is a day to strengthen ties with our living families, do work for those who died without the ordinances of salvation, and write family histories.

10. It is a day for missionary preparation and work. ("The Sabbath: Holy Day or Holiday?" *Ensign*, October 1994, 26–27)

In addition to Elder Didier's observations, many young priesthood holders have been prompted to engage in other activities also appropriate for the Sabbath. Some have sent encouraging letters or e-mails to their friends who belong to other religious faiths. The results have been amazing, with many positive relationships being established.

Others have used part of the day for reading wholesome material and preparing talks and lessons for church and for family home evenings. Many Aaronic Priesthood holders use some of their time on Sunday to play with their younger brothers and sisters, who, of course, are not only a bit surprised but very appreciative. They may even start bragging about what a great brother they have! Sunday is also a wonderful time to talk to Mom and Dad and discuss questions, problems, and concerns that you might have about the gospel or the way your own life is going.

Begin this Sunday to add to your enjoyment, peace of mind, and your spiritual growth by improving the way in which you keep the Sabbath day holy. It may take a little practice and a few adjustments in your lifestyle, but it is well worth it. The Lord will be especially mindful of what you do to improve your observance of the Sabbath day because you are one of his ordained representatives. You hold the priesthood. The Lord will be quick to recognize your good efforts and bless you abundantly.

Chapter 17

How to Keep
the Law of the Fast

If you are a normal human being like the rest of us, when you fast, you get hungry. Actually, that is a good thing, because you'll appreciate the feelings of people in the world who do not have the abundant blessings that you enjoy. However, when we fast, much more than feeling hungry happens. When you fast, you feel yourself gaining a mastery over your appetite. In other words, your body is subject to your will rather than the other way around. Gaining control over your passions and appetites is especially critical during your teenage years when you are developing into a man.

Now that you are a priesthood holder and a fellow servant

of the Lord, your obedience to gospel principles, laws, and practices gives you power to overcome temptations, to use your priesthood authority, and to help others. The Lord said, "There is a law, irrevocably decreed in heaven before the foundations of the world, upon which all blessing are predicated" (D&C 130:20). If you want a blessing, you have to obey the law upon which the blessing is predicated.

One such law that you should obey is the law of the fast. In our day the Lord has said, "Also, I give unto you a commandment that ye shall continue in prayer and *fasting* from this time forth" (D&C 88:76; emphasis added). Fasting is an important way to put you in harmony with the Spirit of the Lord.

A powerful experience related to praying and fasting is recorded in the Book of Mormon and written about in the *Ensign:*

> To his astonishment, Alma met his friends, the sons of Mosiah, as they were returning from their fourteen-year missionary service among the Lamanites. He rejoiced at their faithfulness and at the devotion with which they had served. Earlier Alma and the sons of Mosiah had persecuted members of the Church. But since their conversion, they had become "men of sound understanding" because "they had searched the scriptures diligently" and "had given themselves to much prayer, and fasting; therefore they had . . . the spirit of revelation, and when they taught, they taught with power and authority of God. (Alma 17:2–3)" ("Increasing Our Spirituality through Fasting and Prayer," *Ensign,* June 2001, 61)

What blessings did the sons of Mosiah receive from their prayers and fasting? They became men of *sound understanding,* and they received the *spirit of revelation* so that they could carry out their duties with power and authority. Clearly, when you pray and fast regularly, you draw closer to the Lord, become a man of sound understanding, and are more able to resist temptation and carry out your duties with power and authority.

A complete fast, which includes contributing the cost of abstaining from food and drink for two consecutive meals, makes it possible to see that no one in the Church wants for food. When you fast, give the equivalent amount of food money to the bishop so that your fasting may be complete. With regard to this aspect of fasting, President Marion G. Romney said, "We can, we ought, and we must do better. If we will double our fast offerings we shall increase our prosperity, both spiritually and temporally. This the Lord has promised, this has been the record" ("The Law of the Fast," *Ensign*, November 1974, 14).

Instead of letting Mom and Dad pay fast offerings for you, you may find it more rewarding and fulfilling to take your own money and give it to the bishop to help the poor and the needy. Claim the blessing that President Romney talked about: "If we will double our fast offerings, we shall increase our prosperity, both spiritually and temporally."

Fasting and prayer go together. Fasting is more than starving yourself. Fasting and praying put you more in tune with the influence of the Lord. When you are fasting, you find that it is a blessing to be able to tune out the things of the world, especially the desires of the body, and focus on the things of the Spirit.

When you are fasting and feeling closer to the Lord, listen carefully to the testimonies that are shared during fast and testimony meeting. You may be surprised at the insights and strong feelings that enter your heart when you pay attention to what is happening in fast and testimony meeting. At some point, you may even want to stand up in your quorum, or in an appropriate church meeting, and share your own testimony.

When you bear a testimony of the truth, the Holy Ghost confirms that testimony within your own heart. That is one reason missionaries grow spiritually strong while on their missions. Bearing testimony, combined with keeping the commandments, giving service, and reading the scriptures, brings many blessings to your life, including strengthening your faith, helping you develop power in the priesthood, making you a stronger person, and making fasting much easier.

In the Church, we have a regular fast once a month; a testimony meeting is scheduled on the same Sunday. Every member is encouraged to fast on this first Sunday, unless restricted by health problems. In addition, sometimes members fast at other times for individual reasons, such as a sick or needy family member or friend. Others fast while praying about serious problems. What you find out is that fasting adds intensity and power to your prayers.

Fasting is something you might want to consider when you are concerned enough about certain problems or situations that you want to do more than say a prayer. Going to the Lord in prayer, accompanied by fasting, increases your faith in the Lord and strengthens your attempt to draw upon the powers of heaven.

When you first start fasting, you may not experience all these results. Don't worry about it. Others have felt the same way. One such individual asked this question in the "Questions and Answers" section of the *New Era*: "I know we are encouraged to fast and pray. I've tried fasting, and, frankly, I don't get that much out of it. Why do we do it?"

Notice the good suggestions made in the answer to this question:

> You say that you have tried fasting and didn't get much out of it.
>
> Elder Ifiok E. Okon, a *New Era* reader serving in the Nigeria Aba Mission, offers some good advice. "Fasting is for spiritual upliftment," he writes. "Just as faith without works is dead, fasting without a positive attitude towards it is dead and brings us no rewards." . . .
>
> During your next fast, try these steps:
> • Pray before beginning your fast.
> • Fast with a purpose, and think often about the purpose of your fast.
> • Remain cheerful and patient.

- Offer a prayer of gratitude at the end of your fast.

Fasting, combined with prayer, can be a powerful force in your life. Don't dismiss fasting just because you've tried it once or twice without results. Each month you have the opportunity to join with the other members of your ward in a fast. Next fast Sunday, try beginning your fast with prayer. You can even pray that you'll be able to understand the value of fasting. And pay close attention during testimony meeting. Try to avoid complaining about missing food. And end your fast with a prayer.

Fasting can be a spiritual influence in your life. It can bring you closer to your Heavenly Father. (*New Era,* October 1993, 17)

Fasting requires a little sacrifice on your part, but it is relatively small when compared to the numerous blessings you receive. If you have to, miss only one meal to begin. Then as you gain more control over your body, extend your fast to two meals. When you break your fast, you will have a whole new appreciation for food! But more importantly, you will feel much more at peace with yourself and with the Lord. Answers to your prayers may be more noticeable. And, if you contribute a fast offering, you will feel the joy of contributing something tangible to needy people.

Chapter 18

When to Share Your Testimony

You may be a little hesitant to share your testimony; perhaps you're concerned that others might think you are strange or maybe something you say might offend someone. President Thomas S. Monson, first counselor in the First Presidency, relates an experience in which he was uncertain whether or not to bear his testimony:

> Many years ago I boarded a plane in San Francisco en route to Los Angeles. As I sat down, the seat next to mine was empty. Soon, however, there occupied that seat a most lovely young lady.

As the plane became airborne, I noticed that she was reading a book. As one is wont to do, I glanced at the title: *A Marvelous Work and a Wonder.* I mustered up my courage and said to her, "Excuse me. You must be a Mormon."

She replied, "Oh, no. Why do you ask?"

I said, "Well, you're reading a book written by LeGrand Richards, a very prominent leader of The Church of Jesus Christ of Latter-day Saints."

She responded, "Is that right? A friend gave this book to me, but I don't know much about it. However, it has aroused my curiosity."

I wondered silently, Should I be forward and say more about the Church? The words of the Apostle Peter crossed my mind: "Be ready always to give an answer to every [one] that asketh you a reason of the hope that is in you." I decided that now was the time for me to share my testimony with her. I told her that it had been my privilege years before to assist Elder Richards in printing that book. I mentioned the great missionary spirit of this man and told her of the many thousands of people who had embraced the truth after reading that which he had prepared. ("That All May Hear," *Ensign,* May 1995, 48)

This young lady later joined the Church and thanked President Monson for sharing his testimony of the gospel with her.

If you were baptized when you were eight years old, you may not remember much about what happened that day. Most young people don't. You may remember that Jesus was baptized and that you were trying to be like Jesus and also be baptized. You may also remember that something felt good about being baptized and that you always wanted to keep that same peaceful, warm feeling.

When we are baptized, we make a special covenant with the Lord. Among other things, we covenant to "stand as witnesses of God at all times and in all things, and in all places." You may not remember that covenant, but now that you are older, read Mosiah 18:9 as a reminder. In fact, you may want to read verses 8 through 11, which contain the entire baptismal covenant. As you read these verses, you will remember the joy associated with your baptism and better understand the agreements that you made with the Lord.

Every time you partake of the sacrament, you renew your baptismal covenant by agreeing to (1) take upon you the name of the Son, (2) always remember him, and (3) keep his commandments, which he has given you, that you may always have his Spirit to be with you (see D&C 20:77). In other words, each week as you partake of the sacrament and renew your baptismal covenants, you agree to stand as a witness for the Lord in all things, places, and times. That means at home, at school—whether you are playing football, attending a party, or watching a movie—and at work.

Bearing a witness of Jesus and of the gospel that you know to be true is an important part of being an obedient and faithful member of the Church. And you, as a priesthood holder with authority to represent the Lord in building up his Church, should be especially aware of your opportunities to share your testimony with others. And remember that you don't even have to say, "I would like to bear my testimony." Just say something about the gospel that you feel is true.

Each time you share your testimony, your hearers will be blessed and so will you. At first, you may be a little afraid to share your testimony with others. However, the more you do share your testimony, the easier it will become; pretty soon you will learn how to share your testimony with great confidence and with simple but powerful words.

You may not have a complete testimony of Jesus Christ, Joseph Smith, or the Book of Mormon, but you do have a testimony of some true principles. You know that when you do well, you feel good. When you make mistakes, you feel awful. Bear that testimony every chance you get.

As you experience the truth of honesty, tithing, prayer, faith, serving others, holding the priesthood, and being obedient, share your testimony of those truths. And remember, you don't always have to stand up in a church meeting and say your testimony out loud. You may want to start in a small group, such as a quorum meeting or a chat with close friends. You can also share your testimony while you are giving a talk in church or presenting a lesson or idea in a fireside or quorum meeting.

The main idea is not to be hesitant in sharing your feelings and thoughts about following the Savior. Don't put off sharing your testimony until you have a lightening bolt come down from heaven and strike you on the side of your head!

Rather than worrying about how big or how little your testimony is, simply stand up and start sharing what you do believe. President Brigham Young is reported to have said, "More testimonies are gained on the feet than on the knees praying for them" (The Power of a Testimony," *Ensign,* January 1979, 3). And Elder Boyd K. Packer said, "A testimony is to be found in the bearing of it!" ("The Candle of the Lord," *Ensign,* January 1983, 54).

As you sincerely share your testimony, you have the promise of the Lord that "I will go before your face. I will be on your right hand and on your left, and my Spirit shall be in your hearts, and mine angels round about you, to bear you up" (D&C 84:88). You already hold the keys of the ministering of angels and have the right to receive extraordinary help when you need it to accomplish righteous purposes. You may find out that your testimony is stronger than you thought!

If you feel that you don't have much of a testimony, start today to get a stronger one. You can do this by studying the scriptures, living the principles of the gospel, being honest in all that you do, being friendly and willing to share your time and talents with the needy, showing love and appreciation for all your blessings, dressing and grooming yourself to show what you believe, and bearing your testimony out loud when the opportunity arises.

Your testimony will grow throughout your life if you are willing to work to strengthen it. Be mindful of the inspired words of President Harold B. Lee concerning a testimony:

"Testimony isn't something you have today, and you are going to have always. A testimony is fragile. It is as hard to hold as a moonbeam. It is something you have to recapture every day of your life" ("Testimony," *Ensign,* May 1975, 8).

Is it hard to recapture your testimony every day of your life? No. In fact, it's quite easy. Simply stay on course to (1) study, (2) pray, (3) keep the commandments, (4) resist the temptations and snares of the adversary, and (5) count your many blessings so that the Spirit of the Lord will continue to lift you up and strengthen your testimony.

As a member of the Church and a priesthood holder, you have the opportunity to strengthen the testimony of others and even attract new members into the Church. The way to do this most effectively is by letting your light shine before others that they may see your good works and be led to investigate and live the gospel more fully in their own lives. Bearing your testimony in *word* and in *action* helps others and strengthens your own testimony at the same time. You feel the inspiration of the Lord as you bear your testimony, and this experience adds great power to the priesthood authority that you already have.

Chapter 19

Open the Windows of Heaven

When you have a moment, ask any faithful tithe payer in your ward or in your family what some of the benefits of paying tithing are. You will be surprised at what they tell you. Some will tell you of temporal blessings, while others will tell you of spiritual blessings. Others will tell you of the good savings and spending habits that they have formed while learning how to pay tithing. Most will encourage you to pay your tithing by saying, "When you earn money, pay the Lord first, then save some for yourself, and then pay any necessary bills, expenses, and obligations that you have. You will receive great strength, insight, and blessings. You will never regret paying tithing."

When you go to your meetinghouse on Sunday or for youth activities during the week, notice the various items that need to be in place for regular church activities to occur. Along with heating, lighting, upkeep and repairs, each meetinghouse has numerous manuals and endless supplies that are needed to assist in teaching the gospel and providing appropriate recreation in the cultural halls. Your tithing makes all of this possible, as well as many other projects on which the Church is working.

Hopefully you learned how to pay tithing when you were a young child. Now, exercising priesthood authority, when you pay tithing, you prove to the Lord that you are taking personal responsibility for the success of his work. Paying tithing is not given to you as a direct assignment. This is something that you do voluntarily and is one of the great tests of your personal righteousness.

As you continue to progress in developing power in the priesthood and becoming a more valuable servant of the Lord, you learn that you are as responsible for promoting the work of the Lord and building up his kingdom as the prophet. You are a priesthood holder and a fellow servant with the prophet in carrying out the work of the Lord. The prophet may have broader decision-making responsibility, but you have an awesome responsibility to keep the commandments and focus your efforts on carrying out the directions and duties given to you.

Filling specific assignments given to you by the bishop and your quorum leaders and advisors is a good start, but you can do more. One thing you can do is assume personal responsibility for promoting the gospel and shouldering some of the burden of building up and maintaining the efforts of the Church. One important way to do this is by paying tithing.

One connection between paying tithing and building the Church is with missionary work. Missionaries spread the gospel to the whole world. Missionaries distribute tracts and pamphlets and copies of the Book of Mormon. They receive supervision from a mission headquarters that requires a building, heat, light, and upkeep. Sometimes missionaries use cars, which need to be purchased and kept in good repair. All of this requires support from tithing funds. In a real sense, every ten cents you pay on a dollar earned makes missionary work possible.

Temples are being built at an unprecedented rate. These cost money to construct, maintain, clean, heat, cool, and repair. If your parents search out names of people who have passed on, someone will have to assist them in getting these names ready for temple work. Your tithing helps with these sacred activities.

Some people believe that they can't afford to pay tithing because of other financial obligations. If you feel that way or have friends who think they can't afford to pay tithing, listen to what Elder Henry D. Taylor, a former assistant to the Quorum of the Twelve, said about that issue, "Frequently we hear the expression, 'I can't afford to pay tithing.' Persons who make such statements have not yet learned that they can't afford *not* to pay tithing. There are many members who from experience can and do testify that nine-tenths carefully planned, budgeted, and spent wisely, with the blessings of the Lord, will go much father than ten-tenths spent haphazardly without planning and without the Lord's blessings" ("I Will . . . Pour You Out a Blessing," *Ensign,* May 1974, 107).

Tithing is a commandment with a wonderful promise. The Lord promises that he will "open you the windows of heaven, and pour you out a blessing, that there shall not be room enough to receive it" (Malachi 3:10). You must admit that is one tremendous promise—especially when you think that the Lord created everything and owns everything. He owns the air you breathe and the ground from which you produce food to eat. He owns the material from which you build a house. He created the animals that you use for various purposes, including food. He created the water that you drink when you are thirsty. There isn't anything that the Lord doesn't own. Yet, he makes a promise that if you will give back to him just ten percent of what you make off his ownership of things, he will pour out great blessings upon you!

Your tithing may be ten cents or $10,000; it doesn't make any difference to the Lord, as long as it is an honest tithing. The widow's mite is just as acceptable as a billionaire's dollars. This is a law and a commandment where you can be perfect, and as someone said, "Ten percent tithing equals one hundred percent blessings!" That's not a bad investment from any point of view.

Beyond the temporal blessings that usually accompany the payment of tithing, there are a variety of ways that the Lord can bless you. President Gordon B. Hinckley mentions, "There are many ways in which the Lord can bless us beyond the riches of the world. There is the great boon of health. . . . There is promised in modern revelation a great blessing of wisdom, of knowledge" ("The Second Law of Tithing," *Ensign,* December 1989, 4).

You know that the Lord cannot lie; the Lord always keeps his promises. If you pay an honest tithing and do it willingly, the Lord will truly open the windows of heaven and pour out his blessings upon you. These blessings may come in a financial or temporal way, or they may come in a spiritual way. The promise is that the blessings will be suited to your needs not to your desire for wealth and riches.

The Lord's blessings come in unexpected ways. Sometimes you may recognize them as blessings, and other times you may not. But the one thing that you can count on for sure is that the promises that the Lord makes will always be kept. When you pay your tithing, you assume responsibility for contributing your fair share to carrying on the work of the Lord, through his Church, to the whole world.

The Lord has said, "I, the Lord, am bound when ye do what I say; but when ye do not what I say, ye have no promise" (D&C 82:10). Now it is up to you to have enough faith to pay your tithing on a regular basis and open the windows of heaven so that the Lord may further bless you.

Part III

Sustaining the Power
of the Aaronic Priesthood

Chapter 20

Avoid Cheating, Stealing, and Lying

What is right is right, even if you are the only one doing it.
What is wrong is wrong, even if everyone is doing it.

—Anonymous

Before we address the issue of why we shouldn't cheat, steal, and lie, let's define these terms for you by using a typical dictionary. In each definition, notice if any ideas tempt you.

Cheating is when you deprive someone of something valuable by lying or when you break the rules of a game or a test.

President James E. Faust said, "Cheating in school is a form of self-deception. We go to school to learn. We cheat ourselves when we coast on the efforts and scholarship of someone else" ("Climb High," *New Era*, June 1997, 6). Students who choose not to cheat, and don't allow others to cheat from them, are sometimes called goody-goody, snob, or teacher's pet.

Whether you're at school, playing games, or hanging out with friends, you have to choose what is right even though some of your friends may want you to do differently. If you cheat just once, especially with your friends, it will be hard to say no in the future.

Stealing means to take the property of another wrongfully, to take something from another without right or without detection, or to take something without permission.

Usually stealing starts out by taking little things. We borrow things from people and don't give those things back. Maybe we notice money lying out in the open and are tempted to take a little of it. Sometimes we are tempted to take something without asking because no one seems to be using it regularly. Remember, you hold the priesthood and represent the Lord. You have promised to set a good example in your home, at school, at church, and with your friends. To take something without permission is to dishonor yourself, set a poor example for others, and offend the Spirit of the Lord.

Lying is action marked by or containing falsehoods. To lie is to intentionally make an untrue statement, or to create a false or misleading impression.

One of the bad things about telling a lie is that you have to tell a whole bunch of lies to cover up the first lie. For instance, if you skip out on church and your dad asks you what happened in your deacons quorum meeting, you have to make up a lie because you weren't there. If you say that you had a good lesson and your dad asks you what it was about, you have to lie even more. Usually, we eventually get caught in our lies. And it's not fun. Better to be known as a person who tells the truth and can be trusted.

What do these three acts have in common? Of course, they are all based on *dishonesty* and *deceit*. To be dishonest and deceive is to make others believe that something is true that is false. Deceit and its synonyms all imply leading someone astray or frustrating someone by underhandedness. To deceive implies imposing a false idea or belief on someone that causes ignorance, bewilderment, or helplessness.

What do the scriptures say about people who deceive others, people who lie, steal, and cheat? Mormon, a great prophet from the Book of Mormon, tells us directly what we should do regarding dishonesty and deception: "Turn, all ye Gentiles, from your wicked ways; and repent of your evil doings, of your lyings and deceivings, and of your whoredoms, and of your secret abominations, and your idolatries, and of your murders, and your priestcrafts, and your envyings, and your strifes, and from all your wickedness and abomination" (3 Nephi 30:2).

We learn from this scripture that we should distance ourselves from lying and deception and repent of any lying or deception that we might be involved in. Lying and deception are listed among the worst evils of scriptural times, along with such things as idolatries, murder, and priestcrafts. We can assume that cheating, lying, and stealing—all deceptions—rank high in the evils of this day also.

Why do young people seem to disregard the commandment to avoid these serious sins? The answer is neither absolutely clear nor simple to understand. One would think that these direct and inviolable statements would be heeded without question. Regrettably, apparently young people do not see a direct causal connection between the violation of the commandments and the punishment of lying, cheating, and stealing. What they fail to understand is that consequences will follow—and those consequences will be serious.

We plead with you not to even test the principle that lying, cheating, and stealing have serious consequences. Your eternal life may be at stake. Seriously reflect on this scripture: "There is a law, irrevocably decreed in heaven before the foundations of this world, upon which all blessings are predicated" (D&C 130:20). If you violate laws of righteousness, you will not only miss out on the blessings that the Lord has intended for you, you will also suffer the consequences associated with breaking the law unless you change and repent.

Repentance

If you do break a law of righteousness, don't spend a second trying to rationalize your behavior. Admit to yourself what you have done and get on with the process of repentance. President Spencer W. Kimball explains the process of repentance, which tends to follow five steps: sorrow for sin, abandonment of sin, confession of sin, restitution for sin, and doing the will of the Lord (see *Repentance Brings Forgiveness* [Salt Lake City: The Church of Jesus Christ of Latter-day Saints, 1975], 7–12).

SORROW FOR THE SIN

True sorrow for committing a sin induces a desire to repent. You don't wait until you are caught stealing or lying or cheating. Rather, when you violate one of those laws, you seek out your bishop and start the process of repentance. You feel great sorrow for having engaged in stealing, lying, or cheating.

ABANDON THE SIN

We read in the Book of Mormon that "blessed are they who humble themselves without being compelled to be humble" (Alma 32:16). To abandon a sin means that you stop engaging in that behavior on a permanent basis. In the Doctrine and Covenants, we read, "By this ye may know if a man repenteth of his sins—behold, he will forsake them" (D&C 58:43).

CONFESS THE SIN

The confession of a sin is an important step in repentance. Serious sins must be confessed to a branch president or a bishop, as well as in prayer to the Lord. For serious transgressions, you need at least two sources of forgiveness: (1) that of the Church through its proper authorities and (2) that of the Lord.

The first source of forgiveness is handled by the bishop, who will hear the confession, judge its seriousness, determine the degree of your repentance, and decide whether or not it deserves forgiveness. Forgiveness from the Lord occurs as you follow the remaining two steps.

RESTITUTION FOR THE SIN

If you are humble in sorrow, have completely stopped the behavior that violates the law, and have confessed to Church authorities, your next step is to repair, insofar as possible, any damage that has occurred as a result of your action. For instance, if you have stolen something, you must return it to the rightful owner. Murder and sexual sins have no provisions for total restitution, since you cannot restore life or virtue, but most transgression involving others will require an apology and some kind of damage repair.

Do the Will of the Father

This means that you must be prepared to do good the rest of your life. The Doctrine and Covenants states, "If thou wilt do good, yea, and hold out faithful to the end, thou shalt be saved in the kingdom of God" (D&C 6:13). The good work that you do is taken as evidence that you are living the commandments and have repented.

We all make mistakes. But we can all change and do better. Don't let a sin stand in the way of your progress. President Hinckley has observed that some people think that the quality of character known as honesty is a pretty ordinary subject. "But I believe it to be the very essence of the gospel. Without honesty, our lives and the fabric of our society will disintegrate into ugliness and chaos" ("We Believe in Being Honest," *Ensign*, October 1990, 2).

There is enough cheating, stealing, and lying going on in the world without us adding more to it. Determine now to look over your actions and see if anything you do falls under the heading of dishonesty or deception. If you find yourself doing something that is not right, stop immediately, repent, and strive to do only good things. As President Hinckley says, without honesty our lives will disintegrate into ugliness and chaos.

Chapter 21

Shun the R- and X-rated Things

At a recent priesthood session of general conference, President Hinckley spoke rather directly on a topic he has spoken about before. He said that the matter about which he was going to speak has always been a problem, but "it is a much more serious problem now. It is like a raging storm, destroying individuals and families, utterly ruining what was once wholesome and beautiful. I speak of pornography in all of its manifestations" ("A Tragic Evil among Us," *Ensign,* November 2004, 59).

Like President Hinckley, we'd like to talk directly and boldly about one of the primary causes of bad behavior and immorality—the so-called R- and X-rated things, including movies, magazines, videos, television shows, video games, books, short stories, comic books, radio programs, and Internet displays. Together, these things are called *pornography*.

For one of these media to be called R- or X-rated (NC-17), it must include portrayals of immoral behavior, antisocial behavior, obscenities, and violence. In our view, any material that shows scenes or incidents that are debasing and personally injurious to positive values and to spiritually sensitive individuals are unfit for your consumption and should be avoided. Many PG-13 and some PG movies have scenes and descriptions that distract you from having good thoughts. Vulgar and sordid language is also part of the R- and X-rated scene.

The consequence of being exposed to these pornographic materials is deadly serious. The basic reason for this is that such materials degrade the individual, both male and female. In a conversation published in the *New Era* about pornography and certain kinds of movies, books, and magazines, Dr. Victor Cline, an expert witness before Congress on the effects of pornography and a university professor, offered his views for young people in the Church. He says, "I have reviewed almost all of the published evidence, plus the private commission studies, and I can tell you clearly and simply that there are a number of studies that show high linkages, high statistical correlation, indicating negative results from being exposed to pornography, especially among youth" ("A Conversation on Things of the Spirit, Pornography, and Certain Kinds of Movies, Books, and Magazines," *New Era,* May 1971, 8).

Shun the R- and X-rated things. As Dr. Cline explains, however, "Certainly it's difficult to live in the world and to avoid knowing and seeing what's going on. . . . If you're a sound, active Latter-day Saint, certainly you should be able to keep things in balance and not have your mental and spiritual nature disturbed or affected by these influences. That's the challenge! Simply being in the world presents these challenges to us. I don't see, frankly, how we can avoid them. Even if you read only one of the ten best sellers in fiction, you may run into a problem, for nearly all of them contain a tremendous amount of anti-Christian values. . . . We are indeed living in a corrupt world, and we cannot totally screen out all of these kinds of things. We have to learn to live above them" ("A Conversation on Things of the Spirit, Pornography, and Certain Kinds of Movies, Books, and Magazines," *New Era,* May 1971, 10).

Many publications, such as *Sports Illustrated,* with its illustrated swimsuit issue, may not be considered by most people to be R-rated, but few people can look at the women in bathing suits and immediately feel impressed to thank the Lord for creating such beautiful people. Because these kinds of pictures are titillating, they do great injury to our spiritual receptivity and sensitivity.

President Monson, first counselor in the First Presidency, said, "Some publishers and printers prostitute their presses by printing millions of pieces of pornography each day. No expense is spared. The finest of paper, the spectrum of full color combine to produce a product certain to be read, then read again. Nor are the movie or Web site producer, the television programmer, or the entertainer free from taint. Gone are the restraints of yesteryear. So-called realism is the quest" ("Pornography, the Deadly Carrier," *Ensign,* July 2001, 2).

So what can you do? Dr. Cline urges the following: "Each youth must seek to make his life one of joy, of happiness, of goodness and fulfillment. Read good books and see good movies. Participate in good experiences. And when, in the normal course of events, books and magazines and movies aren't all that they should be, learn to discriminate, to seek the good, and to seek things that are really praiseworthy" ("A Conversation on Things of the Spirit, Pornography, and Certain Kinds of Movies, Books, and Magazines," *New Era,* May 1971, 5).

President Monson admonishes us to return to righteousness, quest for the good life, and pledge to wage and win the war against pernicious permissiveness. He says to choose this day whom you will serve; choose to serve the Lord (Joshua 24:15). He then challenges us to "let our hearts be pure. Let our lives be clean.

Let our voices be heard. Let our actions be felt" ("Pornography, the Deadly Carrier," *Ensign,* July 2001, 3).

As a young priesthood holder, you must face the realities of living in this world and fight the good fight against all kinds of R- and X-rated things, as well as anything else that leads you away from the Lord. You will know when you are viewing, reading, or hearing things of a destructive value in your life because you will feel uncomfortable and guilty.

This is one battle you can win by starting now to avoid any kind of material that distracts you from thinking good thoughts and engaging in wholesome activities. The Lord is on your side. Every really good person is on your side. It is up to you now to wage the good battle and win the great victory. You can do it. We know you can.

Chapter 22

Do the Right Thing at School and in the Community

As a young priesthood holder, you might not have paid much attention to doing the right thing at school or in the community. However, it is one of the most important items you should consider. Why? Because temptations to do the wrong thing are minimal when you are sitting in church with a group of faithful Latter-day Saints. The real test comes when you leave church and get caught up in all the activities of daily living.

Your challenge is to do the good and right things that you learn about in church, outside in the community. This is a rather simple way to show yourself and the Lord that you've "got your act together" and that you are consistent in doing the right thing, no matter where you are.

But there is another important reason that you should do the right thing at school and in the community. You live in schools for much of this part of your life, and you are always part of a community. You may think that what you do is no one else's business, but nothing could be further from the truth. When you behave poorly with another person, you destroy a little piece of your community. When you don't build up someone or something, you rip it down. You do a tremendous disservice to yourself as well as to others who are part of your school and community.

A school or community, even a family or a church, can be torn apart when individuals fail to treat each other properly, tell the truth, and exercise self-control. Doing the right thing involves not only telling the truth but also protecting the integrity of the family unit, respecting others, speaking kindly of others, serving others unselfishly, and preserving the physical well-being of others.

You have already read about Jesus and how he treated everyone with respect. Jesus didn't care whether a person was old or young, rich or poor; whether a person had a title or didn't; whether someone was smart or not; or where a person came from. Jesus treated everyone with kindness and respect; we should try to do the same.

When Spencer W. Kimball served as president of the Church, he took time to visit with prisoners at the Utah State Prison. While he was there, the prisoners wanted to shake his hand and have their pictures taken with him. He smiled, talked with them, and obliged their requests. One observer said that you couldn't tell whether President Kimball was meeting with a group of priesthood holders or a group of prisoners because he treated everyone so well! (Marvin J. Ashton, "The Prophet and the Prison," *Ensign,* May 1980, 35–37).

Elder Richard G. Scott of the Quorum of the Twelve Apostles explains why you should start now to do the right thing wherever you are. He said:

Do what is right even though it seems that you
will be alone in so doing, that you are going to lose
friends, that you will be criticized. What you will
find is that by doing what is right, after a period of
testing, the finest friends will be discovered and you
can mutually support each other in your resolve to
be obedient to all of the commandments of the Lord.
As you learn that truth, you will also discover that
when you have taken a determined stand for right,
when you have established personal standards and
made covenants to keep them, when temptations
come and you act according to your standards, you
will be reinforced and given strength beyond your
own capacity, if that is needed. ("Do What is Right,"
Ensign, June 1997, 51)

As a holder of the Aaronic Priesthood, have a plan or strategy
for doing the right thing. The easiest way to slip away from doing
the right thing is to give in to small violations of key standards.
For instance, it might start by using vulgar language, littering
classrooms and hallways, calling other people names, pushing
and hitting others, making fun of other people, or refusing to
extend common courtesy to other people.

One way to stay on the straight and narrow path is to simply
focus on one moral principle at a time. For example, you could
begin by trying to always speak kindly of others. After you master
this moral principle, following other principles will come more
easily.

Three simple moral behaviors will guide you as you try to do
the right thing at school and in the community: respect others;
speak kindly of others; and serve others unselfishly.

As you read about each of these three fundamental behaviors,
think about which one you would like to focus on first in your
own life.

Respect Others

Just as Jesus did, you have the obligation to respect others
in school and in your community, regardless of their looks or

circumstances. Don't make the mistake of assuming that some of your friends are more important than others or that some of your schoolmates deserve less respect than others. By consistently giving others respect, you are doing the right thing. And when you do right things, you feel better and increase the respect others have for you.

We know a young man of priest age who was quite popular with both boys and girls in his high school. At school dances, he could have danced with the most popular girls in the school, but he demonstrated his respect for all of the girls by dancing with girls who were seldom asked to dance by the popular boys. He received a little heat from his friends on the football team, but he persisted in dancing with a wide range of girls. To this day, he is respected for his courage in resisting the taunts of his classmates, but he also has his own self-respect for doing the right thing.

Show your respect by treating all people like you would treat your best friends. Talk to them, smile, help them when you can, and be polite to them. It only takes a little effort to show your respect to others but the rewards to both you and them are gigantic!

Speak Kindly of Others

One of the easiest things to do is to talk about and spread gossip about some other kids at school or in the community that you don't particularly like. Our mouths probably get us into more trouble than any other part of us. The temptation is almost overwhelming to make a nasty comment about someone with whom you have a disagreement, especially if the other person is saying something bad about you.

As an Aaronic Priesthood holder, you must never give into the urge to speak unkindly of another person, regardless of what they say about you. This is something you can do.

A young man we know was sitting in a meeting with some of his colleagues. During a rather heated discussion of what the group was supposed to be accomplishing, an antagonist of the young man took the floor and berated him mercilessly. The young man sat, quietly listening to the comments, and when the antagonist sat down, the young man simply resumed the conversation without reference to what had been said about him. During a recess, as the young man was walking toward the door, he was surrounded by other members who had attended the meeting. They complimented him for his restraint, saying that the other person was totally out of line. The respect of others and his reputation for being a leader was greatly enlarged.

Serve Others Unselfishly

Of all the odious acts that human beings can inflict on others, one of the worst is selfishness. The synonyms of *selfish* reveal its devilish meaning: greedy, grasping, hoggish, covetous, miserly, churlish, stingy, mean, ungenerous, uncharitable, and egotistic. Few terms have such consistently negative implications. To live life in a selfish mode indicates that a person not only lacks respects for others but also has a great disrespect for self. Selfish people degrade others and try to enhance their own self-regard in the process, but selfishness simply backfires and destroys the selfish person.

A person who holds the Aaronic Priesthood ought to exemplify the highest standard of unselfishness. The synonyms of *unselfish* set a beacon to be followed: generous, openhanded, charitable, noble, high-minded, great-hearted, fair, just, impartial, and unbiased.

You should serve others unselfishly so as to show your generosity, your charity, your nobleness, and your great-heartedness. You should take the lead in giving to others, always seeking ways to honor others, and dealing with others in a fair, just, impartial, and unbiased manner. Err on the side of kindness and high-mindedness and you will always be glad you did.

A young priesthood holder was attending an end-of-school picnic held at the city park. The lunch was served as a buffet on a table where everyone lined up and picked up their food as they walked past the table. Students lined both sides of the table, and some shuffling and shoving occurred as people jostled for a place in line.

As this young man approached the plate on the table holding

delicious-looking cookies, only one cookie remained. He and a fellow student on the other side of the table, a person he didn't particularly like anyway, arrived at the cookie plate at the same time. He had the powerful urge to grab the last cookie and walk away, but he didn't. He paused briefly until the other student picked up the last cookie and walked away without even a nod of recognition. Nevertheless, the young man only smiled and went on his way.

This was a simple act but one that illustrates the enormous power of serving others unselfishly as a way to demonstrate the importance of doing the right thing at school and in the community. That young priesthood holder is making his school and community a better place while developing the power of the Aaronic Priesthood by doing the right thing.

As Elder Scott suggested, start now to do the right thing at your school and in your community. Then follow Elder Eyring's suggestion and pick one of the moral principles that you just read about: respecting others, speaking kindly of others, or serving others unselfishly. Implement the principle in your life immediately. This is one simple experiment where you are assured of a positive result for your good effort.

Chapter 23

Plan to Attend Seminary

Notice the title of this chapter: Plan to Attend Seminary. There are locations in the Church where young people are invited to attend a seminary class when they are as young as twelve years old, but most young people will have to wait until they reach junior high school age. The reason we included this chapter for you as a newly ordained Aaronic Priesthood holder is so you can start planning to attend seminary the first opportunity that you have. Sometimes young men get so busy with the other activities in their lives that they don't take the time to fit seminary classes into their schedules when the opportunity arises.

Let's start with the story of Katie Bliss who, like many young men and women, wondered what her seminary teacher could possibly teach her. Her seminary experience was a bit surprising. This is what she reported:

> I had always just assumed that when you got into ninth grade, you went to seminary. So I was surprised when I received a call from the bishopric asking me if I wanted to enroll. I thought, "Sure. Why not?"
>
> The next thing I knew, it was the first day of ninth grade, and I was on my way to released-time seminary. I was pretty scared and not very excited. "Yeah," I thought, "another church meeting to go to every day. What could my teacher possibly have to teach us every single day? And I was supposed to do this for four years? What if I didn't know anyone in my class? What if I didn't like my teacher? What if I just didn't want to go?"
>
> But I forced myself out the door of my high school and took that long trek to the seminary building. When I got there, I looked for my name to see which class I was in. I then waited for someone I knew so I wouldn't have to be alone. Little did I know that in seminary you are never alone. I finally gave up waiting and went to class. As I walked into the classroom, I was greeted by a warm smile and a friendly handshake. That's when things started to get better.
>
> I took a seat, and as I looked around at all of the beautiful pictures on the walls, my friends started to come in. Friends! Now I could have fun. Class finally started, and we all told a little about ourselves. Then the teacher, Brother Toma, introduced himself and told us about seminary—how important it was to come every day and how there would be gospel study, fun activities, and sometimes even treats!
>
> I couldn't believe how fast that class went by. It was so much fun; I didn't want to leave. When the bell rang, I had to drag myself back to the school.

When I returned to school, I could instantly tell a difference. My school had never seemed so worldly before. I was amazed at how strong the Spirit had been in that seminary building, even on an orientation day.

Besides the daily gospel lessons, there were dances, parties, assemblies, testimony meetings, opening and closing socials, and early-morning devotionals. Those devotionals surprised me the most. I never thought it would be worth it to get up at 6:00 a.m. for a church meeting, but I was wrong." ("Soaking Up Seminary," *New Era*, August 2003, 38)

Like Katie, when you get an opportunity to go to seminary you may wonder whether you should make the effort to attend regularly. Many young people believe that life is stressful and crowded enough without trying to fit seminary into their schedules. The fact is that attending seminary might be one of the smartest and uplifting things that you could possibly do to relax a little and feel the peaceful influence of the Spirit.

Let's see what President Hinckley has to say about taking advantage of this unique gospel educational opportunity: "Take advantage of every opportunity to enlarge your understanding of the gospel. Make the effort to participate in seminary and institute programs" ("Tithing: An Opportunity to Prove Our Faithfulness," *Ensign*, May 1982, 42).

That's about as short and sweet and direct as you can get: a prophet of the Lord has directed you to "make the effort to participate in seminary and institute programs." Additionally, President Hinckley says: "Our great program of Church education moves forward. The work of training students through the seminary and institute program is constantly being enlarged. We urge all for whom it is available to take advantage of it. We do not hesitate to promise that your knowledge of the gospel will be increased, your faith will be strengthened, and you will develop wonderful associations and friendships" ("The Miracle

Made Possible by Faith," *Ensign,* May 1984, 47).

Yes, you may have to get up a little early to attend seminary. And, yes, you may have to juggle your school schedule to keep a time open to take seminary. And, yes, you will have to make sure that you get enough sleep the night before class so that you don't fall asleep during the lesson. So is it worth it?

Darrin Lythgoe, an LDS author and web programmer attended early morning seminary in Massachusetts. He lists several great rewards and growth that come from attending seminary:

TESTIMONY

A personal testimony of the restored Church and the Savior's divine mission is the most valuable knowledge you can gain in this life.

GOOD FRIENDS

You'll get to know other youth from your area who share your beliefs and standards.

BLESSINGS FROM OBEDIENCE

You'll gain deep peace knowing you're doing what your Heavenly Father wants you to do.

SCRIPTURE MASTERY

With a little work, you can learn and better understand the scriptures. Through the scriptures, you can come to know the Savior better.

INSPIRATION

A daily dose of spirituality can open and enlighten your understanding, maybe just when you need it most.

REST

Leave your earthly cares in your locker for an hour. When you're through, your mind will feel clearer.

Spiritual Confidence

With a little study, you'll feel more comfortable discussing gospel topics. You'll also find it easier to answer questions from friends.

Missionary Preparedness

In just a few years, you'll be ready to teach the gospel on your own. Soak it in now—you'll thank yourself later.

Gospel Knowledge

There's so much to learn, from Adam and Eve to Lehi's dream and Joseph Smith's First Vision (see "Idea List: Why Bother with Seminary," *New Era*, September 2001, 33).

When you were first given the Aaronic Priesthood, you may not have had a lot of gospel knowledge. But it was never intended that you should remain uninformed about the powerful principles and doctrines of the gospel and the powers and blessings of the priesthood. If you are to honor the priesthood that you hold, you must strengthen your faith and testimony and learn all that you can about the gospel. When the opportunity presents itself, go to seminary. Attending seminary is a simple way to increase your knowledge of powerful gospel truths. Don't miss this valuable opportunity, even if it takes a little extra effort on your part. Ask your parents for help if you need it to make proper arrangements for your attendance at seminary. You have everything to gain and absolutely nothing to lose!

Chapter 24

Moving Ahead with Poise and Confidence

The spiritual condition of a man is determined by the degree to which he honors, in his life, the priesthood which has been conferred upon him.
—President Rudger Clawson

The order of the priesthood has existed from the foundation of the world—being without beginning of days or end of years, from eternity to eternity (see Alma 13:3). "Wherefore, now let every man learn his duty, and to act in the office in which he is appointed, in all *diligence*" (D&C 107:99; emphasis added).

This is your moment!

Now that you understand more about the tremendous powers and blessings of the Aaronic Priesthood, you get to decide to what extent you want to honor your priesthood, magnify your calling, enlarge the potential of your priesthood, and proceed forward with poise and confidence. You can also choose to not pay much attention to the priesthood and stagger around on wobbly legs in a bit of confusion.

No one can decide for you. You must decide to what extent you will put into practice in your life the principles, powers, and keys of the Aaronic Priesthood. Because you are a young man and have the opportunity of holding the priesthood, President Rudger Clawson is right when he said that your whole spiritual condition depends on the degree to which you honor your priesthood.

You know by now that the priesthood is not vocational or professional. You can't go to school and receive the priesthood for completing course work. The priesthood is not hereditary or offered for money. It is not held by a group of religious scholars. You do not receive the priesthood because you are a government magistrate, member of a famous family, or a popular person in your neighborhood.

The priesthood has been revealed from heaven. You receive the priesthood because you are a worthy member of The Church of Jesus Christ of Latter-day Saints. Men are called to the priesthood because of their exceeding faith and righteousness before God.

If you would really like to know what the Lord has in mind for you, read slowly this prophetic statement about you that is recorded in Joel and repeated by Peter:

"And it shall come to pass afterward, that I will pour out my Spirit upon all flesh; and your sons and your daughters shall prophesy, [and] your old men shall dream dreams [and] your young men shall see visions" (Joel 2:28; see also Acts 2:17).

Elder Henry B. Eyring of the Quorum of the Twelve Apostles recently told a group of parents that those things are happening right now. "That scripture does not say that your sons and your daughters may claim the gift of prophecy by the Spirit. It says that they will. It doesn't say that your young men may see visions. It says that they will. And it will come because the Lord will pour out His Spirit upon all flesh" (CES Satellite Training Broadcast, August 2004).

This is what the Lord has in mind for you. If you are worthy, the Lord will bless you with the gift of prophecy and you will see visions. In short, the Lord will share more and more of his priesthood authority and power with you; he will lead you with personal revelation and visions; and he will give you the spirit of prophecy. The Lord's Spirit is being poured out upon you, but you must choose whether or not you will receive it.

To use the priesthood keys of the ministering of angels and the full power of the Aaronic Priesthood, and to receive inspiration, visions, and directions from the Lord as recorded in Joel, you must be humble, prayerful, and led by the Holy Spirit; you must become meek, submissive, patient, full of love, and long-suffering. You must have faith in the Lord and show by your good works that you are ready to receive his great power and blessings.

You must learn how to enjoy yourself and have fun but put aside childish acts that are inappropriate to one who holds power and authority from God to represent him. You must learn quickly that you don't just hold the priesthood while you are in church. You hold the priesthood while at school, in your home, or hanging out with your friends.

President Hinckley, a prophet of God, appeals to you directly:

> I plead with you, I ask you to live worthy of the tremendous thing which you have. You do not need to be prudes. You do not need to be self-righteous. You cannot be arrogant in any way. But you can be humble, living decently and cleanly, as you serve the Lord as one holding the priesthood after the order of Aaron. The Lord expects that we will keep our lives in order, that we will live the gospel in every aspect, that we will shun evil and not partake of the "mean and beggarly" elements of life. ("Priesthood Restored Directly from Heaven," *Church News*, May 22, 2004, 3)

Sometimes you may think that you are a little young to step

up to the plate and hit a home run. You are not. When you are young and become a deacon is the perfect time to live right and claim the blessings of the priesthood and all the blessings that Elder Eyring pointed out.

Marvin O. Ashton, counselor to the Presiding Bishop from 1938 to 1946, spoke often to the young men of the Church and to their parents. In one of his quiet sermons, he made the point that the characters of people are created when they are young and that these characters are revealed as people mature. Bishop Ashton pointed out that James Watt, inventor of the first steam engine, was a sickly little fellow at home with nothing to do but "throttle the throat of a steaming tea kettle to see it explode its lid. . . . The seed was there as a boy, and afterwards developed into the man inventor" (*To Whom It May Concern* [Salt Lake City: Bookcraft, 1955], 94).

Bishop Ashton noted that at age twelve, Ulysses S. Grant, the general who brought the Civil War to a close and became president of the United States, would go into the mountains, "drag on logs, bind them with chains, and deliver the wood home without help of an adult." Thomas Edison, inventor of the electric light and a hundred other inventions, was found as a lad "in the middle of the night, when his folks were asleep, electrocuting cockroaches on the kitchen floor." Florence Nightingale, who started the Red Cross, began her nursing career "as a little girl in helping a lame dog she found on the road from school" (*To Whom It May Concern*, 94–95).

All these extraordinary people started young to develop the talents and blessings that were given to them. Bishop Ashton's point is that you need to acquire the spirit and the perseverance and the dedication to live the gospel and honor the priesthood when you are young, so that it might reveal itself more fully as you grow a little older.

That's what your parents, priesthood advisors, and bishop are trying to do—instill the principles and practices of the Aaronic Priesthood in you while you're young, so that you will grow into a confident, faithful person who is ready to receive the Melchizedek

Priesthood when you're older.

You have learned by now that it takes a little determination on your part and a whole lot of patience to reap the rewards of honoring the Aaronic Priesthood. As you move forward in your life as a priesthood holder, you will hit smooth spots and rough spots. Don't worry about it. That's how life is. Very little that is great or significant happens in a single day.

Occasionally you will have a high moment when everything seems like it is going well. However, for the most part you will wonder whether you are making any kind of real progress in your life.

Have you ever noticed how the dew settles on the dry grass at night so that in the morning it looks like someone watered the lawn? You wonder, when you awake to a new day, how the dry grass suddenly became wet! That's how most of our significant learning takes place. We study and study, and suddenly— seemingly overnight—we understand.

Listen to what the Lord says about your confidence, your priesthood, and the dew from heaven: "Let thy bowels [interior parts] also be full of charity towards all men, and to the household of faith, and let virtue garnish thy thoughts unceasingly; then shall thy confidence wax strong in the presence of God; and the doctrine of the priesthood shall distil upon they soul as the dews from heaven" (D&C 121:45).

Be faithful. All the power, blessings, and rewards of honoring the priesthood will distill upon you as the dews from heaven. Your confidence will wax strong. The Lord never fails to keep his promises. As you move through this challenging period of your life from deacon to priest, try your very best not to fail at being worthy to receive the Lord's promised blessings, which include his love and the comforting outpouring of his Spirit.

Index

Magnify callings: by keeping commandments, 76; Lord's help with, 29; Lord's promise for, 42; through sharing gospel, 28; through service, 44

Melchizedek Priesthood: authority of, 3; preparation for, 5, 28, 130

Missionary service: builds kingdom of God, 100; preparation for, 20, 28–29, 30, 85, 125; worthiness for, 34

Monson, Thomas S.: on pornography, 113; on sacredness of Aaronic priesthood, 4; on testimony, 93–94

Nelson, Russell M., on prayer, 57

Nonmember friends, 17, 33

Obedience: blessings of, 19–20, 78–79, 124; to God's law, 88; to inspiration, 66–67; to parents, 70; to priesthood leaders, 44, 45–46

Obligation, 32, 117

Packer, Boyd K.: on development, 7–8; on inspiration, 63; on quorum membership, 36; on testimony, 96; on youth, 11

Parents: communicating with, 70–71, 72; help from, 4; honoring, 70

Peterson, H. Burke, on priesthood authority and power, 50–51

Pornography, 111–14

Prayer: answers to, 64–65; avoid temptation through, 58–59; for direction, 59–60; improving quality of, 60–61; manner of, 59

Priesthood: administrative offices of, 44; advancement in, 5, 11, 42; honoring, 125; order of, 127, 129; power of, 49–50; succession, 15

Quorum: meetings, 16, 37, 44; membership, 36, 38; organization, 35–36; presidency, 36, 43–44, 45

Repentance, process of, 108–9

Respect: for God, 58; for leaders, 43–44, 45–46; for others, 41, 116–17, 118, 120; for sacred ordinances, 41–42

Revelation: divine, 77, 81, 102; personal, 66–67, 129; spirit of, 89

Right: doing, 3, 11, 16, 42, 115–16, 117–18, 120; and wrong, 9, 70–71

Romney, Marion G., on fasting, 89

About the Authors

Eric G. Stephan is a professor emeritus of organizational leadership at Brigham Young University. A popular speaker and author, he has made presentations at BYU Campus Education Week and at Know Your Religion programs throughout the United States.

Eric has served as a high councilor, bishop, branch president, and stake executive secretary. He and his wife, Sandra, are the parents of seven children and a group of wonderful grandchildren.

R. Wayne Pace, professor emeritus of organizational leadership at Brigham Young University, has served as president of the Academy of Human Resource Development and of the International Communication Association.

Wayne has served as a high councilor, stake director of teacher development, and councilor in a bishopric. He and his wife, Gae, are the parents of six children, several grandchildren, and a few great-grandchildren.